THE DIARY
of
DR. CHALONER CLAY

THE DIARY OF THE VOYAGE TO AUSTRALIA ON BOARD THE SAILING SHIP 'HESPERUS' IN THE YEAR 1881

Edited by
Robert Snow

THE DIARY OF DR. CHALONER CLAY

The Diary Of The Voyage To Australia
On Board The Sailing Ship 'Hesperus'
In The Year 1881

Edited by Robert Snow

First edition published in 2016 by FLYING DISK PRESS

FLYING DISK PRESS
4 St Michaels Avenue
Pontefract
West Yorkshire
England
WF8 4QX

Published by
FLYING DISK PRESS

Designed and typeset by: Bob Tibbitts (iSET)

Cover artwork by Matthew Oliver

ISBN 978-0-9934928-1-5

Copyright © 2016 Robert Snow. All rights reserved.
Without limiting the rights under copyright reserved above, no part of this publication
may be reproduced, stored in or introduced into a retrieval system, or transmitted
in any form by any means (electronic, mechanical, photocopying, recording or otherwise),
without the prior written permission of both the copyright owners
and the publishers of this book.

THE DIARY OF
DR. CHALONER CLAY

Dr Chaloner Clay is in the centre of this picture

THE DIARY OF DR. CHALONER CLAY

DR Chaloner Clay was born in 1858 in the Manor House at Fovant in the county of Wiltshire. He was the son of Dr. Robert Richard Clay and as he was only 23 years of age at the time of the voyage to Australia he must have only just qualified in medicine.

The reason for the long voyage was to help him recover from consumption – at the start of the journey he was in very poor health but it seems that after the voyage his health was much improved. Dr. Clay Died in 1916 at his home, the Manor House in Fovant.

The "*HESPERUS*" was a clipper and was constructed of iron. She was built by Robert Steele & Co. at Greenock in 1873. She had a gross tonnage of 1859 and was 262.2ft in length. She was owned by Anderson, Anderson & Co. and her port of registry was Aberdeen. The master is shown to be T. R. Harry at the time of the voyage.

In 1891 the vessel was bought by Devitt & Moore to be used for a cadet training scheme. In 1899 she was sold to the Trustees of Odessa Commercial School and her name was changed to "*GRAND DUCHESS MARIA NIKOLLAEVNA*", port of registry then became Odessa.

In 1921 she was sold to the London Steamship & Trading Corporation and was renamed "*SILVANA*". In 1922 her ownership changed to S. Bertorello and Ricardi. Finally the vessel was broken up in 1924.

From Lloyds Register of Shipping

HESPERUS

An iron fullrigged ship built in 1873 by Robert Steele & Co., Greenock. Dimensions: 262'2"×39'7"×23'5" and tonnage: 1859 GRT, 1777 NRT and 1574 tons under deck. Equipped with two decks and the forecastle was 40' long and the poop 74'. Sister ship to the same owner's [?] ship *Aurora*. Originally rigged with skysails.

1873 November

Launched at the shipyard of Robert Steele & Co., Greenock, for the Orient Line (Anderson, Anderson & Co.), Aberdeen. Assigned the official British Reg. No. 68500 and signal MNDL. Employed in the Australian trade.

1873-1875 November

In command of Captain John Legoe.

1875-1877

In command of Captain Wm. Cummings.

1876

Sailed from London to Adelaide in 80 days.

1877

In command of Captain T.R. Harry.

c1890

In command of Captain Cook[e].

1890

Sold to Devitt & Moore, London, to be used as a sail training ship.

1890-1898

In command of Captain J.H. Barrett late of the same owner's ship Rodney.

1890 October 1

Sailed from London to Sydney in 91 days.

1891 September 11 - December 8

Sailed from London to Sydney in 88 days.

1892

Sailed from Sydney to London in 86 days. This was her first voyage home by way of Cape Horn.

1892 October 11 - December 23

Sailed from London to Sydney in 73 days from Lizard Point.

1893 September 11 - December 29

Sailed from London to Hobson's Bay, 72 days from the Lizard Point. On December 10 the Hesperus logged 358 miles.

1898-1899

In command of Captain Charles Maitland late of the same owner's ship Harbinger.

1899

Sold to Russian owners in Odessa for £9,000 and was renamed Grand Duchess Maria Nikolaevna.

1913

Refitted by Swan and Hunter, Wallsend.

1921

Sold to London Steamship and Trading Corporation and was renamed Silvana.

1924

Broken up at Genoa.

Robert Steele & Co.

GREENOCK

Yard closed in 1883.

IRON SHIPS

Yard No.	Launched	Name	Tonnage	Type
1	1854-09	Beaver	266 reg	SS
2	1855-02	City of Madras	914 reg	ship.
3	1855-03	Plover	382 reg	SS
4	1855-06	City of Quebec	664 reg	ship.
5	1855-07	City of Dublin	814 reg	ship.
6	1855-08	Mangerton	364 reg	SS
7	1856-01	City of Tanjore	799 reg	ship.
8	1856-03	Inca	230 reg	PS
9	1856-08	Dom Affonso	240 reg	SS
10	1856-09	Panther	442 reg	PS
11	1856-09	cargo float	600 BM	cargo float
12	?	Dom Pedro	244 reg	SS
13	1857-04	Scotia	1021 reg	SS
14	1857-06	United Kingdom	1067 reg	SS
15	1857-08	City of Canton	909 gross	ship.

16	1858-04	*Palestine*	936 reg	ship.
17	1858-09	for River Ganges	1346 BM	PS
18	1858-11	---	680 BM	cargo float
19	1859-05	---	871 BM	cargo float
20	1859-06	---	871 BM	cargo float
21	1859-12	*Canadian*	1310 reg	SS
22	1861-03	*City of Hankow*	241 reg	SS
23	1861-08	*St George*	1141 reg	SS
24	1861-05	---	271 BM	dredger
25	1862-04	*Circe*	71 reg	schooner yacht.
26	1862-04	*Sarah*	161 reg	SS
27	1862-06	*Reverie*	24 reg	schooner yacht.
28	1862-07	*E. Shun*	288 reg	schooner.
29	1862-09	*Silvercraig*	491 reg	barque.
30	1862-11	*King Arthur*	700 reg	ship.
31	1863-01	*Waverly*	1000 reg	ship.
32	1863-08	*Peruvian*	1908 reg	SS
33	1863-03	*Tuh Shing*	275 reg	schooner.
34	?	---	---	iron barge
35	?	*Barwon*	311 reg	SS
36	1863-04	---	776 BM	steam lighter.
37	1863-12	*Taeping*	757 reg	composite clipper ship.
38	1864-02	*Lady Palmerston*	1247 reg	ship.
39	1864-09	*Redgauntlet*	1073 reg	ship.
40	1864-09	*Arundel Castle*	1042 reg	ship.

41	1864-07	Moravian	1598 reg	SS
42	1864-10	Knight of Snowdoun	656 reg	ship.
43	1864-11	Lord of the Isles	656 reg	ship.
44	1865-03	Tantallon Castle	1057 reg	ship.
45	1865-07	Aglaia	31 reg	schooner yacht.
159	1865-07	Sir Lancelot	886 reg	composite clipper ship.
46-51	1865-10	---	---	180ft long hopper barges.
58	?	---	---	iron bow for hopper barges.
52	1866-01	Ravenscrag	1263 reg	ship.
53	1866-06	Janet Cowan	1278 reg	ship.
54	1866-09	Gryfe	1073 reg	ship.
55	1866-12	City of Athens	1199 reg	ship.
56	1867-02	Pomona	1196 reg	ship.
57	1867-04	Fleetwood	650 reg	ship.
59	1867-09	Ardgowan	1283 reg	ship.
60	1868-02	Cartsburn	1257 reg	ship.
61	1868-04	Walter Baine	898 reg	ship.
62	1868-06	Ralston	815 reg	ship.
63	1868-07	Hartsfield	815 reg	ship.
64	1868-08	Assaye	1281 reg	ship.
65	1868-09	Parsee	1281 reg	ship.
66	1868-10	Araby Maid	837 reg	ship.
67	1868-12	Lake Superior	1274 reg	ship.

68	1869-03	*Halcione*	843 reg	ship.
69	1869-11	*Scandinavian*	1701 reg	SS
70	1869-10	*Cathcart*	1387 reg	ship.
71	1869-11	*Ladyburn*	1431 reg	ship.
72	1869-07	*Arethusa*	1272 reg	ship.
73	1870-06	*Palatine*	192 reg	yacht.
74	1871-03	*Samaritan*	2316 reg	SS
75	1872-02	*Polynesia*	2032 reg	SS
76	1871-07	*Lake Simcoe*	350 reg	barque.
77	1872-06	*Circassian*	1484 reg	SS
78	?	---	551 BM	iron barge
79	1873-04	*Brimschweig*	2085 reg	SS
80	1873-09	*Numberg*	2085 reg	SS
81	1874-06	*Sardinian*	2577 reg	SS
82	**1873-11**	***Hesperus***	**1777 reg**	**ship.**
83	1874-07	*Eurydice*	1465 reg	ship.
84	1874-09	*Aurora*	1768 reg	ship.
85	1874-11	*Orpheus*	1462 reg	ship.
86	1874-12	*Niobe*	1469 reg	ship.
87	1875-04	*Bannockburn*	1675 reg	ship.
88	1875-06	*Lady Ruthven*	1591 reg	ship.
89	1875-07	*Bencleuch*	1350 reg	ship.
90	1875-09	*Zingara*	263 reg	yacht.
91	1875-06	*Cuba*	112 reg	barge.
92	1875-11	*City of Santiago*	1296 reg	SS
93	1875-11	*Deveron*	1256 reg	ship.
94	1875-11	*Aline*	718 reg	barque.
...	...	...	...	...
170	1883-09	*Inveruglas*	--	---

The Hesperus at sea.

The Hesperus at her moorings.

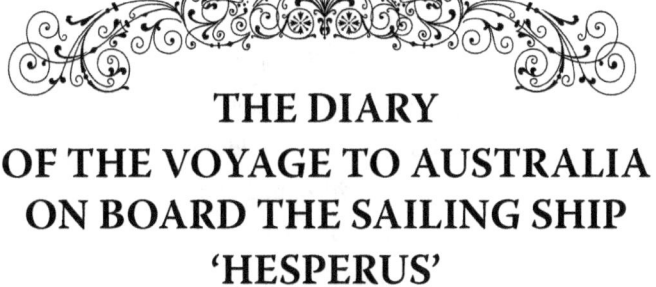

THE DIARY
OF THE VOYAGE TO AUSTRALIA
ON BOARD THE SAILING SHIP
'HESPERUS'
IN THE YEAR 1881

Transcribed from the original Diary
by **Robert M. Snow,** Great Grandson of Dr Chaloner Clay

Kept by Dr. Chaloner Clay

VOYAGE TO AUSTRALIA

Ship:- 'Hesperus'
Skipper:- Captain Harry
Surgeon:- Mr. Mallam
Crew 37

Passengers
20 Saloon.
20 Second Class.
60 Steerage.

Saloon Passengers

Mr. & Mrs. Lerick
Mr. & Mrs. Collier
Mr. & Mrs. Young
Mrs. Gibbs & 2 Children
Mrs. Miss. & young Roland
Mr. Drysdale
Mr. Beywell
Mr. Marmion
Mr. Colgan
Mr. Binks
Mr. Pemberton
Mr. Hoyer

Thursday July 21st. 1881.

Slept at The Half Moon last night and embarked about 5pm. Was to have sailed yesterday.

Friday July 22nd.

Two tugs took us out of the basin of South Dock at a quarter to 6am this morning, arrived at Gravesend about 12.30am, when a doctor came and inspected all the crew, and the Ships Husband Captain Andrews introduced me to the Skipper. We took up a few passengers, a cow, sheep, pigs, fowls (old hens), ducks and geese, it was great fun especially with the Porkey animals, who ran about deck, so there was a chase after them. I sent a letter home from here. We cast anchor for the night in the hove.

Saturday July 23rd.

Weighed anchor at 4.30 this morning and tugs took us down the channel, nasty head wind blowing all the while and very cold. Arrived off Dover at 3pm. Off Dungeness about 7pm and passed Hastings at 10pm.

Sunday July 24th.

Arrived off the Isle of Wight about 3pm. Tugs did not leave us until 4pm when the sails were set, guns fired and the Skipper took charge of the vessel. The tugs were obliged to come so far on account of the head wind. Chopping sea on fire, Saloon passengers absent from dinner owing to the Sea Fever.

Monday July 25th.

Tossed about a bit, keep on tacking, head wind still. Needles still in sight. Viewed the French Coast this afternoon. Sea Fever still very virulent. Half the Saloon passengers are shooting cats and in the steerage a mother has to mind her 11 children; in another family the mother and five out of 7 children are shooting cats. I have not felt the least inconvenience from the movement of the vessel. The surgeon is an old good man who has been in practice, and is taking this voyage to benefit his health, he is a jolly fellow.

Tuesday July 26th.

We are at last out of sight of land and a jolly breeze has sprung up, sailing at 8 1/2 knots, the Skipper is now in his glory. A stowaway gave himself up after being hid forward in the hold.

Wednesday July 27th.

In the bay becalmed, unusual, the sea is as smooth as a lake.

Thursday July 28th.

Jolly breeze again, 8 knots an hour but on the wrong course.

Friday July 29th.

Saw a shoal of porpoises, the great lazy animals kept rolling over as if it was a great exertion to them, also saw some of Mother Carey's chicken (Storm Petrels), they are much like a swallow, with curved beak and webbed feet. Thermometer 60 degrees in Saloon.

Saturday July 30th.

Sailing at 8 knots, most of the invalids are better. Several passengers going out to farm, one old Lincolnshire farmer told me, that out of the 16 years he had had his farm he had lost money 11 out of the sixteen years so he is going to try Australia.

Sunday July 31st.

Rather rough last night, rain and wind tossed about a good deal, consequently the passengers are upset again. Did not have church, geese let out on deck to get a washing.

Monday August 1st.

Fair wind, we are now on proper course at last. Beautifully warm, sun hot. I took 3 grammes of Henbane but did not sleep.

Tuesday August 2nd.

Calm sea and hot sun, I took 2 1/2 grammes of Chloral last night.

Distance: 76 miles.

Latitude.44 degrees-3 north.

Longitude.14 degrees-33 west.

Wednesday August 3rd.

Dancing on poop last night. Misty morning, which cleared up and sun came out hot. Grand fun to see two of the ladies boxing, regular windmill affair at first, but one of them learnt to hit out and gave her opponent some capital straight ones.

Distance: 99 miles.

Latitude 43 degrees 52 north.

Longitude 16 degrees 27 west.

Thursday August 4th.

My companion kept me awake the whole night by swearing and cursing the B--- Flats and then he got out of his bunk and rubbed Laudanum into his arms and legs until he upset the bottle, so I had the port and door open, he kept his lively game up all night. Fine this morning with sun, rain in the afternoon. Had some singing this evening.

Distance: 144 miles.

Latitude 143 degrees 35 north.

Longitude 19 degrees 46 west.

Friday August 5th.

Fine morning with wind aft, just the thing. Hard rain in evening.

Distance 94 miles.

Latitude 42 degrees 9 north.

Longitude 20 degrees 34 west.

Saturday August 6th.

Smooth sea, fine evening, showery in afternoon.

Distance 154 miles.

Latitude 39 degrees 38 north.

Longitude 21 degrees 14 west.

Sunday August 7th.

Going along smoothly, sun strong off the coast of Lisbon. Had church in the Saloon for first time, fair attendance. Flying fish seen as ship crossed our bow.

Distance 162 miles.

Latitude 30 degrees 51 north.

Longitude 21 degrees 14 west.

Monday August 8th.

Still fine. Do not feel up to much.

Distance 139 miles.

Latitude 30 degrees 51 north.

Longitude 23 degrees 10 west.

Tuesday August 9th.

Going at 6 knots, warm with but little sun. Passengers getting tired of seeing nothing but blue water. Off Madeira about 260 miles distance.

Distance 165 miles.

Latitude 32 degrees 7 north

Longitude 23 degrees 53 west

Wednesday August 10th.

In the North Trades. Had toothache last night, did not sleep.

Distance 165 miles.

Latitude 29 degrees 31 north.

Longitude 24 degrees 55 west.

Thursday August 11th.

Saw a shoal of flying fish, they do not fly very far at a time. We are having condensed water now which is very good. They condense from 4 to 5 hundred gallons daily. Sea has been very smooth for last few days. Sun very scorching. Thermometer in sun 90 degrees Fahrenheit.

Distance 132 miles.

Latitude 27 degrees 40 north.

Longitude 25 degrees 50 west.

Friday August 12th.

Slept in saloon last night as cabin was so stuffy. Saw some kind of duck.

Distance 110 miles.

Latitude 27 degrees 40 north.

Longitude 25 degrees 50 west.

Saturday August 13th.

Sunset and moon rising very pretty. We reached the tropics about 2pm. Plenty of flying fish knocking about.

Evening Amusements.

Singing hymns and chants at the stern part of the saloon and playing nap at the fore part. Jolly breeze sprung up.

Distance 140 miles.

Latitude 23 degrees 45 north

Longitude 27 degrees 49 west.

Sunday August 14th.

Had a large congregation at church this morning. Sea alive with flying fish. Not very hot as there is a nice breeze.

Distance 177 miles.

Latitude 20 degrees 52 north.

Longitude 28 degrees 14 west.

Monday August 15th.

I slept in the saloon on the floor.

Distance 197 miles.

Latitude 17 degrees 24 north.

Longitude 29 degrees 0 west.

Tuesday August 16th.

Very close and depressing, air being so moist. A homeward bound vessel passed on the starboard side. A flying fish flew on deck and was caught, very pretty. Hardly moving.

Distance 138 miles.

Latitude 15 degrees 24 north.

Longitude 29 degrees 22 west.

Had some acting and a concert on the poop which was covered and decorated with flags. The acting was very good. Mr. O'Connor played the violin beautifully, he is a professional. It all went off very well.

Programme

The Merchant of Venice Trial scene

Portia:- Mr. Latimer.
Shylock:- Mr. Read (2nd mate).
Basanio:- Mr. Marmion.
The Duke:- Dr Mallam.
Nerissa:- Miss Ebbs.
Antonio:- Mr. Brett.
Gratianio:- Mr. Ebbs.

Overture	Lucretia Borgia.	Mr. O'Connor and Mrs. Thurston.
Song	In the Gloaming.	Mrs. Young.
Recitation	Nancy Brigg.	Mr. Pucket (3rd mate)
Fantasia	Scotch Aus.	Mr. O'Connor and Mr. Thurston.
Song	The girl in a Pinafore Dress.	Mr. Irvin.
The Penny Showman		Mr. Collyer.
Pianoforte		Miss Ebbs.
Song		Nancy Lee.

God Save The Queen.

Wednesday August 17th.

Several vessels sighted today. Becalmed, lifeboat lowered for a row. The doctor had a nasty squeeze, the boat as the wares swung her up caught his legs between it and the side of the ship. Very close lightening in the evening.

Distance 51 miles.

Latitude 14 degrees 56 north.

Longitude 29 degrees 2 west.

Thursday August 18th.

Still becalmed, boat again lowered, very hot, sun blistered those who were in the boat pretty well. Saw some large black fish (10 or 12 feet long) and very much like a whale. Temperature in the sun 124 degrees fahrenheit, in the shade 94 degrees fahrenheit.

Distance 43 miles.

Latitude 13 degrees 56 north.

Longitude 28 degrees 30 west.

Friday August 19th.

Very queer last night, cough very troublesome, saw a large shoal of albacores and porpoises close to the vessel, the albacores jump very high out of the water. Fair wind not so hot, but little sun. The phosphorous in the sea of an evening very pretty.

Distance 100 miles.

Latitude 12 degrees 16 north.

Longitude 28 degrees 48 west.

Saturday August 20th.

Becalmed again, the boat was lowered and as they were getting on board again they lost the rudder, so some of the sailors had to pull some distance astern for it. Temperature in the sun 93 degrees fahrenheit. Saw a shark at stern of vessel about 8 or 9 feet long. They tried to catch him but could not. More albacores, porpoises and flying fish.

Distance 41 miles.

Latitude 11 degrees 36 north.

Longitude 28 degrees 39 west.

Sunday August 21st.

Becalmed in morning. Squalls in afternoon and wet.

Distance 32 miles.

Latitude 11 degrees 04 north.

Longitude 26 degrees 39 west.

Monday August 22nd.

Not much wind, air warm and moist and consequently very prostrating. I feel it very much indeed. A steamer passed this evening, could see her lights.

Distance 73 miles.

Latitude 10 degrees 13 north.

Longitude 27 degrees 47 west.

Tuesday August 23rd.

Spoke the 'Otoga' at 5 am. homeward bound from New Zealand, after dinner we signaled the 'Francis', we dipped the ensign three times and she replied.

Distance 118 miles.

Latitude 9 degrees 19 north.

Longitude 26 degrees 02 north.

Wednesday August 24th.

Beautiful breeze on going at 11 knots. Air warm and damp, rain in the evening.

Distance 142 miles.

Latitude 9 degrees 27 north.

Longitude 26 degrees 02 west.

Thursday August 25th.

Still going well. Saw some Bosun (Boatswain) very pretty birds. Very seedy had a bad night.

Distance 198 miles.

Latitude 7 degrees 27 north.

Longitude 21 degrees 23 west.

Friday August 26th.

Spoke the 'Aethuopia' from London, outward bound.

Distance 154 miles.

Latitude 5 degrees 28 north.

Longitude 19 degrees 01 west.

Saturday August 27th.

Lot of flying fish. Sun hot with cool breeze. Had a game of cribbage with the doctor and then round with him to see his patients.

Distance 142 miles.

Latitude 4 degrees 46 north.

Longitude 24 degrees 107 west.

Sunday August 28th.

Slept beautifully last night and was jolly and cool.

Distance 174 miles.

Latitude 3 degrees 43 north.

Longitude 24 degrees 0 west.

Monday August 29th.

Last night Father Neptune came on board with music playing (tin cans and a beater), he paraded the deck and shook hands with all the passengers and then called our names over and requested the pleasure of seeing us tomorrow at 2 pm.

Distance 171 miles.

Latitude 2 degrees 6 north.

Longitude 26 degrees 20 west.

Tuesday 30th August.

Saw some Nautilis this morning of a light pink colour with their sails up, looked very pretty. Crossed the Equator and at 2 pm. Father Neptune and his wife accompanied by the Doctor and the barber and suite, the Police went round serving everyone with a summons to appear before his Majesty or they would be fined, I paid the fine. Three of the saloon passengers underwent the operation, which was, first the Doctor saw him and accordingly doctored, him with dough and cayenne pepper pills when he put out his tongue, plaster over his mouth, ears and eyes, consisting of treacle some of which is painted over face and head, he is then lathered with a mixture of bran and oil and put on with a large brush like a white washing brush, some of which is poured over head and chest, he is then shaved with a wooden razor as large as a sword, which keeps coming in contact with his nose. His hair is next brushed with a large brush used for sweeping with the handle taken out. The Bears then collar him and draw him into a sail with about 4 feet of water and duck him well. After they were all finished Neptune and his Wife parade the deck and 'Auld Lang Syne' and 'Rule Britannia' finished the performance. Caught 9 rats in the hold.

Distance 218 miles.

Latitude 0 degrees 0 south.

Longitude 28 degrees 0 west.

Wednesday August 31st.

Good breeze, going well, vessel pitching like fun. Caught a lot more rats down in the hold.

Distance 170 miles.

Latitude 2 degrees 19 south.

Longitude 29 degrees 43 west.

Thursday September 1st.

Going at 10 knots an hour. Saw some of Mother Carey's chicken again.

Distance 208 miles.

Latitude 5 degrees 47 south.

Longitude 30 degrees 3 west.

Friday September 2nd.

Wind fresh, with a heavy sea on. Keep on washing over the deck. Very close in saloon and cabins, as we are obliged to keep our ports shut. A lot of passengers knocked up again.

Distance 210 miles.

Latitude 9 degrees 10 south.

Longitude 30 degrees 46 west.

Saturday September 3rd.

Going at 10 1/2 knots an hour. Sunrise very pretty this morning. Sea very jolly, waves washing over deck.

Distance 218 miles.

Latitude 12 degrees 28 south.

Longitude 32 degrees 23 west.

Sunday September 4th.

Wind and sea same as yesterday. Did not have service.

Distance 248 miles.

Latitude 16 degrees 14 south.

Longitude 35 degrees 2 west.

Monday September 5th.

Rough night, quieter this morning.

Distance 246 miles.

Latitude 20 degrees 15 south.

Longitude 35 degrees 2 west.

Tuesday September 6th.

Going at 12 1/2 knots last night, but this morning only 4 knots, wind having dropped. Now out of tropics.

Distance 211 miles.

Latitude 23 degrees 45 south.

Longitude 34 degrees 42 west.

Wednesday September 7th.

Put up the strong sails yesterday as some of the other were torn by the wind. A homeward bound vessel passed us this morning. Speed 8 knots.

Distance 165 miles.

Latitude 26 degrees 20 south.

Longitude 33 degrees 40 west.

Thursday September 8th.

Very cold, obliged to put on an overcoat. A lot more Cape pigeons flying about the vessel, they are black and white with curved beak and webbed feet, also some Cape hens which are larger than the pigeons and black. Passed an outward bound vessel, was going to signal only a squall came on.

Distance 160 miles.

Latitude 27 degrees 27 south.

Longitude 30 degrees 57 west.

Friday September 9th.

Signalled the 'Timaru' from Glasgow, bound for Otago, New Zealand, left the same day as we did, viz. July 22nd. Not much wind. Sea very pretty.

Distance 186 miles.

Latitude 28 degrees 11 south.

Longitude 27 degrees 31 west.

Saturday September 10th.

Saw an albatross and some mollyhawks. While in the tropics we saw no good sunsets as I expected, but this evening the sunset was beautiful.

Distance 119 miles.

Latitude 28 degrees 51 south.

Longitude 25 degrees 23 west.

Sunday September 11th.

Three Cape pigeons were caught, they were sea sick directly they got on board. Ship rolled very much last night, which kept me awake. We are obliged to plug ourselves in our bunks. Did not have church.

Distance 49 miles.

Latitude 29 degrees 20 south.

Longitude 24 degrees 37 west.

Monday September 12th.

'Timaru' still in sight.

Distance 155 miles.

Latitude 31 degrees 11 south.

Longitude 22 degrees 32 west.

Tuesday September 13th.

We have left the 'Timaru' behind now a breeze has sprung up, she kept in sight for two days. Lightening very vivid this evening.

Distance 165 miles.

Latitude 33 degrees 29 south.

Longitude 20 degrees 40 west.

Wednesday September 14th.

Very cold. Going at 11 1/2 knots this morning.

Distance 198 miles.

Latitude 35 degrees 48 south.

Longitude 17 degrees 52 west.

Thursday September 15th.
A mollyhawk caught today, it measured from wing to wing 7 feet.

Distance 148 miles.

Latitude 39 degrees 13 south.

Longitude 13 degrees 24 west.

Friday September 16th.
Captain is steering for Goffs Island. Two whales passed close to vessel while we were having dinner. Morning damp and misty.

Distance 148 miles.

Latitude 39 degrees 13 south.

Longitude 13 degrees 24 west.

Saturday September 17th.
This morning early Goffs Island was sighted, and we passed close by it, it is a high mountain of rock of a good height, with shrubs on the top and a little stream of water running down the sides. A lot of birds followed from the island but were too wary to be caught. Speed 8 knots. The Skipper caught an albatross, it measured from the tip of one wing to the tip of the other 9 feet 3 inches. The breast is used for muffs, the feet for tobacco pouches and the bones in each wing for pipe stems.

The highest peak at Goffs Island is 4,385 feet. The other islets are very pretty, especially the one known as the church which bears a close resemblance to one.

Distance 201 miles.

Latitude 40 degrees 12 south.

Longitude 9 degrees 14 west.

Sunday September 18th.

No service. Beautifully warm in the morning, but damp and cold in the evening. The sunset was magnificent this evening, all shades of yellow, blue, red and green.

Distance 143 miles.

Latitude 40 degrees 54 south.

Longitude 6 degrees 13 west.

Monday September 19th.

Very misty and cold. Wind freshening.

Distance 166 miles.

Latitude 41 degrees 50 south.

Longitude 2 degrees 46 west.

Tuesday September 20th.

Still misty and damp. Thermometer 49 degrees fahrenheit. Water 47 degrees fahrenheit. Began our run eastward.

Distance 212 miles.

Latitude 42 degrees 31 south.

Longitude 1 degree 54 east.

Wednesday September 21st.

Sea pretty, going along 11 knots an hour. A tremendous number of whale birds about this morning, they are about the size of a dove, grey colour with very pointed wings and a band of black across each wing which meets in the middle back at an acute angle. Ship very steady, air fresh and bracing.

Distance 285 miles.

Latitude 42 degrees 30 south.

Longitude 8 degrees 17 east.

Thursday September 22nd.

Speed 14 1/2 knots last night and 12 knots this morning.

Distance 303 miles.

Latitude 42 degrees 39 south.

Longitude 15 degrees 8 east.

Friday September 23rd.

Round the cape last night in calm weather; this is not the usual Cape weather. Several Cape pigeons caught. Very cold.

Distance 246 miles.

Latitude 42 degrees 53 south.

Longitude 26 degrees 04 east.

Saturday September 24th.

Sun warm but wind cold. I have been a good deal better since we have been out of the tropics.

Distance 234 miles.

Latitude 42 degrees 53 south.

Longitude 26 degrees 04 east.

Sunday September 25th.

Very cold. Vessel rolled very much last night which prevented me from sleeping. No service today on account of the rolling. Sunset very pretty.

Distance 138 miles.

Latitude 42 degrees 58 south.

Longitude 29 degrees 12 east.

Monday September 26th.

Wind very cold. Thermometer 44 degrees fahrenheit only.

Distance 138 miles.

Latitude 43 degrees 32 south.

Longitude 34 degrees 15 east.

Tuesday September 27th.

Going at 12 1/2 knots. Nothing going on but cards.

Distance 269 miles.

Latitude 43 degrees 83 south.

Longitude 45 degrees 14 east.

Wednesday September 28th.

Going very slowly. More Cape pigeons caught. Still very cold. Thermometer 45 degrees fahrenheit in the saloon, but only 38 degrees fahrenheit on the poop. Had hail this afternoon with wind.

Distance 212 miles.

Latitude 42 degrees 57 south.

Longitude 45 degrees 14 east.

Thursday September 29th.

Distance 126 miles.

Latitude 41 degrees 46 south.

Longitude 47 degrees 34 east.

Friday September 30th.

It is a good deal warmer than it has been for the last 5 or 6 days.

Distance 206 miles.

Latitude 41 degrees 57 south.

Longitude 52 degrees 13 east.

Saturday October 1st.

Hardly moving during the night, so that the vessel rolled very much. This morning wind aft, going along at 10 knots an hour. Pretty good swell on. Weather very nice and generally a good deal rougher.

Distance 172 miles.

Latitude 42 degrees 12 south.

Longitude 57 degrees 3 west.

Sunday October 2nd.

Rolling tremendously last night, and kept most of us awake, consequently several were absent from breakfast. Good wind, going at between 14 and 15 knots per hour. Warm night. Very beautiful sea. Much warmer 60 degrees fahrenheit in saloon. One of Mother Carey's chicken caught yesterday but was let go again. Sea very rough, only the topsails left up, the rest taken in. I had an ugly fall when on the poop, my legs slipped from under me and I fell on my back and shook myself a great deal.

Distance 273 miles.

Latitude 42 degrees 38 south.

Longitude 63 degrees 9 east.

The Storm Petrel, or Mother Carey's chicken is a small, web footed bird, much like the swallow when on the wing with a curved beak, they can easily stand and run on the water and when any refuse is thrown overboard they spread out their long wings and just touch the water.

Monday October 3rd.

Very rough last night, the bathroom washed from near the gangway up to the forecastle and on the main deck the water was very nearly knee deep. The Doctor had a nasty fall on the back of his head. West wind fresh and cold. Sea came into Saloon.

Distance 281 miles.

Latitude 42 degrees 9 south.

Longitude 69 degrees 27 east.

Tuesday October 4th.

Not going so fast today. More Cape pigeons caught. I made a screen for one of the passengers with the head and wings of one.

Distance 216 miles.

Latitude 42 degrees 9 south.

Longitude 69 degrees 27 east.

Wednesday October 5th.

Going but slowly last night but this morning early the wind sprung up and we are going along at the rate of 15 knots an hour. Sea high and very beautiful, to see the spray blown from the crest of the waves. This is the fastest the vessel has been. The log line broke this morning, this makes the second during the voyage.

Distance 357 miles.

Latitude 42 degrees 27 south.

Longitude 82 degrees 13 east.

Thursday October 6th.

Still going very fast, sea same as yesterday.

Distance 313 miles.

Latitude 43 degrees 1 south.

Longitude 89 degrees 19 east.

Friday October 7th.
Very damp on deck, sea breaking over poop. Wind still fresh. Ropes put round deck for supports.

Saturday October 8th.
Have not been on deck for two days on account of damp and cold. Heavy swell on. A good deal of rolling.

Distance 181 miles.

Latitude 42 degrees 32 south.

Longitude 100 degrees 53 east.

Sunday October 9th.
This morning fine and bracing going at about 6 knots. Two mollyhawks yesterday. No service.Very cold.

Distance 185 miles.

Latitude 42 degrees 49 south.

Longitude 106 degrees 17 east.

Monday October 10th.
A beautiful white albatross caught today, it measured from tip of one wing to the tip of the other 11 feet, caught with a hook with a large piece of pork attached to it, it took three or four persons to haul him in. Wind changed, going too much north, going between 6 and 7 knots an hour, fine and bracing. During last Wednesday, Thursday and Friday we did a 1000 knots, a tremendous run which is seldom done. Saturday a folding up chair shut up while I was sitting in it and squeezed two fingers of my left hand and one of my right and I could not get them out until the chair was opened. South wind very cold.

Distance 154 miles.

Latitude 38 degrees 48 south.

Longitude 106 degrees 17 east.

Tuesday October 11th.

Lying to, waiting for a favourable wind. A mollyhawk caught.

Distance 184 miles.

Latitude 37 degrees 38 south.

Longitude 107 degrees 19 east.

Wednesday October 12th.

Very cold going south west. Five mollyhawks caught. I skinned one for Mr. Gibbs.

Distance 121 miles.

Latitude 39 degrees 37 south.

Longitude 106 degrees 48 east.

Thursday October 13th.

Dead calm all day. Sea like glass and as calm as a mill pond. The boat was lowered and some of the passengers shot 5 mollyhawks. Several whales quite close to the vessel and keep on spouting. Have caught cold, very queer.

Distance 5 miles.

Latitude 39 degrees 45 south.

Longitude 106 degrees 45 east.

Friday October 14th.

Little wind. On our proper course fairly warm. This kind of weather very unusual for this latitude. Two more mollyhawks caught today. There is a very pretty grey gull flying about this morning, tip of wings grey and black.

Distance 67 miles.

Latitude 39 degrees 40 south.

Longitude 108 degrees 12 east.

Saturday October 15th.

Going along better. Ship Steady.

Distance 161 miles.

Latitude 39 degrees 32 south.

Longitude 111 degrees 0 east.

Sunday October 16th.

Becalmed again, sea without a ripple. A lot of diving hawks close under the counter, they dive down several feet under the water for the food. Had service, very small congregation. Beautifully warm and dry out. Ship very quiet last night. We are now off Cape Lenivin and may expect fine weather.

Distance 103 miles.

Latitude 39 degrees 8 south.

Longitude 113 degrees 18 east.

Monday October 17th.

Still becalmed, boat lowered. A large whale came close to ship. Sun hot. Cleaning and painting ship for shore. In the afternoon a shoal of whales kept spouting, looked pretty in the distance.

Distance 98 miles.

Latitude 39 degrees 48 south.

Longitude 115 degrees 34 east.

Tuesday October 18th.

Becalmed again. Two albatrosses caught, the one was a beautiful white one measuring from wing to wing 10 feet six inches, the other a very pretty white and grey one. I preserved the head of one of the albatross and also skinned a mollyhawk and preserved the head as well. I have done several heads for the passengers which appears to be all the go now I have started it.

Distance 96 miles.

Latitude 39 degrees 7 south.

Longitude 117 degrees 30 east.

Wednesday October 19th.

Becalmed in morning. Just moving in the afternoon. A fine white albatross caught, similar to the one caught yesterday, it measured from wing to wing 10 feet 4 inches. Morning warm, afternoon rainy.

Distance 90 miles.

Latitude 39 degrees 0 south.

Longitude 119 degrees 26 east.

Thursday October 20th.

Warm with but little breeze. Several mollyhawks caught today. The ship begins to look more like herself with the fresh paint and varnish. One sheep and four pigs left. During the voyage 25 old hens died a natural death and no doubt saved many of the passengers from indigestion as the others were very tough. Going very slowly.

Distance 46 miles.

Latitude 39 degrees 18 south.

Longitude 120 degrees 21 east.

Friday October 21st.

Fair wind at last. Air warm.

Distance 98 miles.

Latitude 40 degrees 10 south.

Longitude 122 degrees 10 east.

Saturday October 22nd.
Very cold, going south. Bad wind again.

Distance 114 miles.

Latitude 40 degrees 45 south.

Longitude 124 degrees 34 east.

Sunday October 23rd.
Had service, very few came, going north. Keep on tacking. Very cold Several huge great whales close to the vessel. Glass still high, up to 31, has been high during nearly whole voyage.

The last sheep killed today.

Distance 105 miles.

Latitude 41 degrees 25 south.

Longitude 126 degrees 40 east.

Monday October 24th.
On our proper course, expect to get to Semaphore next Thursday.

Distance 12 miles.

Latitude 41 degrees 38 south.

Longitude 127 degrees 33 east.

Tuesday October 25th.
On our course in the morning, but wind went round in afternoon.

Distance 169 miles.

Latitude 39 degrees 44 south.

Longitude 131 degrees 2 east.

Wednesday October 26th.

Wretched head wind, the skipper never remembers such weather as this, generally too much wind. The average passage of this vessel is 75 to 78 days and now we shall be 3 weeks late. Last Monday there was great excitement on account of Mrs. Gibbs, giving birth to a fine boy. Two fine albatross caught. today.

Distance 70 miles.

Latitude 36 degrees 37 south.

Longitude 131 degrees 27 east.

Thursday October 27th.

Going north west instead of north east.

Distance 123 miles.

Latitude 36 degrees 44 south.

Longitude 130 degrees 24 east.

Friday October 28th.

Fair wind last night and this morning wrong. Warm but air very moist and sticky.

Have been on board 14 weeks today. A shark was close alongside of the vessel, a line was put out for him but without effect, he was too wary. The sunset was splendid this morning, the sea was without a ripple and about a dozen beautiful albatrosses close in under the counter, with their rainbows of beautiful shades parallel to one another and the shadow of the ship reflected on the water, it was beyond description. Six of the albatrosses were caught, they were like a lot of swans on a pond and fought and growled over the bait, being so hungry.

Distance 69 miles.

Latitude 36 degrees 16 south.

Longitude 132 degrees 8 east.

Saturday October 29th.

Fair wind, hope to sight Cape Border tomorrow. I preserved and stuffed two heads of albatrosses for passengers, have done about 20 altogether.

Distance 66 miles.

Latitude 36 degrees 19 south.

Longitude 133 degrees 30 east.

Sunday October 30th.

Had service this morning. Fair wind. Have been 100 days at sea. Cape Borva's light sighted at 6 pm this evening, it is a revolving light, red and white alternating, seen every minute, the white is visible 30 miles, the red for 15 miles. I went to a tea party in the Captain's cabin. A shark seen.

Distance 108 miles.

Latitude 36 degrees 7 south.

Longitude 135 degrees 42 east.

Monday October 31st.

This morning Kangaroo Island on starboard side and a little distance from it is Cape Jarvis with Backstaus Passage between the two, on the port side is York Peninsula. I am almost sorry to see land, as we are now nearly at the end of our voyage. A large shoal of Porpoises tumbling about close alongside of vessel. The engineer harpooned one, it was about five feet long of a shiny blackish purple colour and white on the underside, snout and inside like a pig, its teeth interlock when the jaws are closed, so that once a fish is in its jaws it cannot escape. About 6.30 pm. the Captain began to clew up the sails and hoisted the Ensign and Company's flags, about 7 pm the pilot, Doctor and Customs Officer came on board. The anchor was dropped at 7.25 pm at the Semaphore. The sunset was grand and Adelaide with the hills behind it and the sun shining on the windows looked very jolly. The 'Abernore' a homeward bound vessel was anchored in the Semaphore, they gave three cheers which was answered by our crew. She starts tomorrow.

Tuesday November 1st.

A steam tug came alongside ship about 2 pm. when we left the jolly old 'Hesperus'. All the sailors went aft and gave three cheers as we steamed away. I was very sorry to leave the old ship, but not to leave the majority of the passengers. The port of Adelaide is a very dirty place.

AUSTRALIA

WHERE the rivers are without fish, flowers are without smell, birds are without song and some also odd people without conscience. Whether that is the case I cannot say, where tis summer when winter in the old country, where the north wind is hot and the south cold, where there is a monstrous animal with a tail as big as a bed post, (makes good soup) with a head like a rabbit and as tall as a grenadier, hopping along as if he had the giants 7 league boots on. Then there is another curiosity in the shape of an animal which is as lazy as a cat, colour and skin of a mole, a bill and web feet of duck, it is a kind of beast, fish and reptile (Platypus). Pigs are fattened on peaches and new milk, thousands of sheep and oxen are boiled down for the sake of their tallow.

The forest trees are evergreen and are chiefly Eucalyptae, native firs and Acacias, but they ought to be called nevergreen or extra brown with the exception of the Acacia and Weeping Willow.

FRUIT GARDENS AND ORCHARDS

Strawberry, Melon, Pumpkin, Tomato, Egg-Apple, nuts (Filberts), Peaches, Nectarines, Apricots, Plums (many different kinds), Cherries, Grapes, Figs, Mulberries, Mangoes, Lemon, Citrus Pomegranates, Currants, Gooseberries, Raspberries, Apples, Pears, Bananas, Quinces and Loquats.

A native dance is called a Conobory, drinking goes on to a great extent. The working man as a rule does not drink while he works, but let them get their wages and go away for a "spell", they will drink as no English man drinks, they will drink down in about a fortnight the earnings of a year. There is less of this with miners, than with the shearers and ploughmen, the miners gamble.

There is a very great jealously existing between the Colonies, one Colony says anything it can against its neighbour although a good many Colonists have never left their own to judge for themselves.

NATIVES

About middle size, the well fed ones fairly proportioned, but the other badly, face broad, nose flat, mouth very large, lips thick, cheek bones high, forehead low, teeth white and large. They are superstitious, courageous, revengeful, dirty, cunning, lazy, great liars and thieves, will eat anything, inside of fish and such like. House rent dear, meat very cheap, butter and milk in the cities the same price as at home and yet there is such a lot wasted up the country. Railway charges are very high. Labour is very dear in the cities and a long distance up the country, but between these labour about the same as in England. Chinese labour is however cheaper and it is chiefly Chinamen employed in Vineries on account of being good gardeners and they are also cheaper.

COLONIALS

They are very fond of sport of any kind, they are also very loyal. As a rule they are tall, about the average height, some slim, others well made, that all have, both men and women a washed out appearance, they are not exactly pale, but more of a sallow, which certainly does not add to their personal appearance, taken as a whole they cannot boast of beauty. Everybody rides, the butcher, the post boy, and all, and go cantering along everywhere, they never trot.

The law of equality is the same in all the colonies.

> *Your Butcher, your Baker.*
> *Your Chandler, your Draper.*
> *All cut the same caper.*
> *And all are on a level with you.*

Servants are at a premium, they want 2 or 3 days out during the week to go and take music lessons, or go to a dance. I know a servant that actually asked her master to buy her a lock and chain for her neck, she said I don't mind giving 4 or 5 pounds for it.

AUSTRALIA

The people out here have meat three times a day, that is with their Breakfast, Luncheon and Tea. The meat however is very inferior to that of the old country, it has very little taste without it has been kept too long.

Vegetables also are fine out here but are very watery and tasteless as also are the fruits with a very few exceptions, oranges, grapes and etc.

The boys out here are paid too well, they know not the value of money and spend it in drink mostly.

Amongst the lighter classics the boys often dictate to their father and think their opinion is the best, it is born in them, it is a great pity.

All people come for is the making of money and when they have it they get regular misers, some, yes many up country there who are rolling in money, but they nor their sons, can read or write and from being so out in the world they are more like savages.

Many persons perish up the country for want of medical aid. Medical fees are very high, which are generally paid for before starting.

Flies are a great nuisance, they congregate round you by hundreds and if you kill them there are plenty that attends his funeral.

Mosquitoes are very large and wont they just bite, but the flies are very nearly as tormenting. In New South Wales the locusts are very numerous and the noise is quite deafening.

The scenery is very beautiful, but it can't come up to that of the old country at the various seasons of the year, out here it is all much after the same style, there is none of the colouring which the trees have at home in the spring and again in the autumn, here they are mostly of a rusty brown colour.

Up the country the horses are not shod and are only fed on the grass, which is burnt up, but they will do their 30, 40, or 50 miles and have nothing but what they can get for themselves, this sun burnt grass is very sweet and there must be a lot of nutrition in it, for the cattle fatten on it.

The Police are mostly Irishmen, but they have a very bad name out here, it is said they are great thieves, most of them have property.

The Railways, Trams and a good many of the Busses belong to the Government.

SOUTH AUSTRALIA

ADELAIDE

Streets are fine, very wide and clean. Some of the buildings are very fine, especially The Town Hall and Post Office, the latter being something to be proud of. The suburbs are very pretty, including North Adelaide, Mitcham and Kensington, the houses are only one storey high with a Verandah all round and a pretty garden in front full of flowers and often little fountains playing in the centre, the houses have flat roofs. There is plenty of dust, hot winds and dust storms, the latter being called 'Brickfielders', and they try a man's temper very severely.

CLIMATE

It is hotter than Sydney or Melbourne, but is dry, so that you can bear it a good deal better without being fatigued, it is delightful.

The Toireus which used to be an almost dry creek, has been dammed up and there is now a large sheet of water on which a number of boats may be seen.

It is called the city of churches and also the farinaceouse City. Chief products wheat and wool. There are copper mines in South Australia, the chief being, Wallaroo, Monta, Kapunda and Buna Buna, Western Australia has lead mines. There has been little gold found in South Australia, and it is thought that eventually there will be a good more discovered, as the wise acres say that it is Anniferous.

The people are more hospitable than in the other colonies.

The frogs give a concert every night, but you can have even too much of a good thing.

NEW SOUTH WALES

SYDNEY

It has the finest harbour in the world, the coast line of it measuring 1500 miles and is full of bays and inlets. It is a magnificent site from the Heads to the Wharf, it is like a grand panorama, it is something well worth being proud of, there is splendid fleet of steamers come to Sydney. The Orient line, P & O, Frisco Mails and Money Wigwams besides a crowd of Sailing Vessels. The streets are narrow and dirty looking and the buildings for the most part unpretending, there are some very good.

The businesses are carried out in a much quieter way than in Melbourne and there is plenty of money in Sydney, but the people as a rule won't invest.

Land at present is very dear and there is a regular mania with those people who have any land of their own cutting it up into very small allotments and getting good prices. A piece of land was sold the other day in George Street, the person who sold it cleared a good [POUND]90,000 in 18 months. Cooger another day will be a fashionable watering place and land will be very dear there.

The people still show the convict blood that is in them, many of the Sydney nobility are descended from them, so that it is a dangerous topic to hit upon.

There is a great lot of sugar grown in New South Wales.

CLIMATE

The climate in Sydney in summer is very bad, being a sub-tropical heat, moist and very depressing, there are even hundreds of old colonists obliged to go out of Sydney for the summer.

They have the steam train that is not supposed to go faster than 8 miles an hour, but directly they get out of the city they do, they are very dangerous. It is astounding the number of Larrikins there are who won't work and who are a terror to the Police and people, they are those low breed people descending of the convicts.

Sydney has gold, coal and copper in the west New South Wales and tin in the north.

VICTORIA

MELBOURNE

It is built on a square, the streets running North, South, East and West. They are very wide like those of Adelaide and trees are planted down some of them. The buildings are very good and beat Sydney but there is a drawback to this and that is its sanitary arrangements, they have open sewage running by side of street and sometimes of a morning the smell is very bad, but I dare say it will be improved before long as Melbourne has sprung to what it is in a little more than 40 years.

Its two staple articles of commerce are gold and wool. The chief gold mine being those Sandhurst and Ballarat.

CHINESE IN MELBOURNE

Labouring classes are fond of gambling and opium smoking, but are industrious, they will carry heavy burdens all through the hottest day of summer without appearing to be fatigued, they are good traders and excellent gardeners, many are married to European women. This is the "Heathen Chinese".

A new arrival from England is called a "New Chum".

CLIMATE

Is very changeable, one day scorching hot, next day cold (I had fires in December then in the summer) another time it may be fine in the morning and soaking in the afternoon, generally good deal of wind, sometimes they get a warm wind for 3 days and then a Southerly breeze springs up. It is however a drier climate than Sydney.

Melbourne is after the Yankee style. The people are a go ahead set rushing about as if they had not a moment to loose. The people are gayer, go in for amusements greatly and dress loud and are very enthusiastic over any games etc.

There is a good deal of wool comes from Sydney, but they say it does not pay to make it into blankets, labouring being dear, although they have protection. There are more manufacturies wanted out here, but their labour is very dear and they have no coal.

The River Yana spoils Melbourne, it is horribly foul and there is plenty of dredging to be done.

The streets being so wide and there also being so many nice gardens, viz. Carlton, Wagstaff, Fitzroy, Treasury and many more, all in town as it were makes it look so open and no doubt makes it very healthy and it would be more so if they would look at their sanitary arrangements.

DIARY WHILE IN AUSTRALIA 1881

Tuesday November 1st.

When we arrived at Port Adelaide, I went with Mr. and Mrs. Lerick to Adelaide City and from there we went to the Terminus Hotel, close by, it was quite a treat to get things fresh. The houses are mostly one storey high with flat roof and verandah, all round, they are very comfortable. There are more public houses or rather hotels as they call them, than anything else. Hay making is now going on strongly, and the sun is beautiful unlike the old country. The horses are very slim, and fine legs and long tails, but they go along well and can endure a lot. The streets quite astonish one, they are a tremendous width, I have never seen anything like them before.

Wednesday November 2nd.

After breakfast went to the Post Office which is a beautiful building, the clock is just like Big Ben at home and the chimes are exactly like Big Ben. Met Mr. Drysdale, Brett and Mrs. Collyer. The people are a very independent set and Jack is as good as his master. The host and hostess sat down to dinner. The Greneig Railway runs along the middle of the streets and there is a man at the end of each carriage to manage the brake, they run at 6 or 7 miles an hour, a bell tingling the whole time. Soquats are in season now, they look much like an apple only with a stone in the centre, they have a very pleasant tart taste.

Thursday November 3rd.

Lerick taken queer, had to attend to him.

Friday November 4th.

Went to Stilling & Co. Orient Line agents and arranged to go by the "Cuzco" expected in next Friday, Dr. Mallam going by same vessel. In the morning went to the Botanical Gardens, they were very lovely, the Geraniums are like shrubs, and some of them are standards and tied up to a stake like a rose tree. The foliage of the trees was grand, and there were any amount of English plants. Also some animals and birds. Met Mr. Drysdale, Miss Roland and her sister and the Skipper at York. In the afternoon Mallam and I took a train to Kensington passing through Norwood and walked out into the country which was very enjoyable. The houses there are pretty little one storey ones with gardens in front full of flowers.

Saturday November 5th.

I went to North Adelaide which is a charming place, the houses are larger here, and the gardens are one mass of flowers and often a little fountain playing in the centre, the trees are crowded with green fruit the vines are grown in the form of a currant bush not trained and are loaded with fruit. Dr. and Brett called today. Sent letter by the 'Chuinborazo

Sunday November 6th.

Went to St. Peters Cathedral at North Adelaide (not finished yet). Choral service just the same as at St. Pauls at home, the singing was very good indeed. In the afternoon Doctor and I went to the Museum at the Institute, which is not very good, there is also a good reading room and library at the Institute.

Monday November 7th.

Went to Stilling & Co. and arranged to have my luggage taken off the 'Hesperus' and transferred to the 'Cuzco'. Went to Mitcham by train, it is under the hills. After dinner went to the Port.

Tuesday November 8th.

Weighed at the station, weighed 10 stone 2 pounds. In the afternoon Lerick and myself went to Orington and called on the Rolands. Mrs. Drysdale left for Mount Gambia.

Wednesday November 9th.

Saw a lot of Colonial Volunteers drill, can't be compared with our home ones. Lerick gone to the Athletic Sports.

Thursday November 10th.

Went to the supreme Court and The Attorney General, Chief Justice Way was sitting. A pair of horses in a cart ran away and smashed the cart all to pieces.

Friday November 11th.

Doctor and I went to the Hospital and saw Miss Beecher who is a trifle better, but there is not the least chance of recovery.

Saturday November 12th.

Mr. and Mrs. Lerick embarked on board the P & O steamer 'Bohilla' for Sydney. I went to Glenely with them and came back with Mallam, who had luncheon with me. Sparrows are a great nuisance here and the government give 2/6d. for every hundred eggs and they have already paid [POUND]40,000. this season. An old Scotch farmer dined here yesterday and he said he had just had 200,000. Shawn, he is one of the largest sheep farmers in the colony, one of his daughters is married to a Judge in Adelaide, the Judge was sweet on the second daughter and wanted to marry her, but old McCullock who had an eye to business said you must take the eldest first and so he did, and had any amount of money with her. The Holdfast Bay and Glenely Railway runs for the most part along the middle of the road. Very warm, lying down all afternoon with my coat, waistcoat, collar and shirt off.

Sunday November 13th.

'Cuzco' expected last Friday, has not been sighted off Cape Borda yet. Very close, had a thunder storm in afternoon which cleared the air.

Monday November 14th.

'Cuzco' arrived this morning. I left Adelaide by the train for the Semaphore Jetty, arrived on board just in time for luncheon, Mallam came a little later. At 6.15 pm the anchor was weighed and away we went, passing Cape Jervis and Cape Willoughby about 9 pm going along Backstaus Passage. The 'Cuzco' is a very decent vessel with about 400 passengers including about 16 or 17 Nuns and a dozen Priests or Fathers, most of them bound for New Zealand.

Tuesday November 15th.

Uneventful day nothing happening much.

Wednesday November 16th.

MELBOURNE

Cast anchor about 10.30 am. after a quick run of 40 hours. Most of passengers left here, those bound for Sydney being afraid of small pox. Four large steamers passed us while we were at anchor viz. The 'Tambora' and The 'Ringarooma' for New Zealand. 'The City of Adelaide' for Sydney and the Orient mail boat 'The John Elder' for England, the ensign was dipped as they passed. Have a cabin to myself now.

Thursday November 17th.

Do not start before tomorrow as there is a very heavy swell on and cargo can't be discharged until tomorrow, therefore shall not get away until mid-day.

Friday November 16th.

Anchor weighed and we steamed away at 1.40 pm. The coast about Queens Cliff is very pretty and thickly wooded.

Saturday 19th November.

Passed Wilson's Promontory about 4 am.

Sunday November 20th.

SYDNEY

Passed the Heads about 2.pm, the pilot came on board and from there to the anchorage was like a grand Panorama, the sun was shining as we entered and the sight was indescribable, well worth coming on to Sydney to see. Raining hard in evening.

Monday November 21st.

Went along by side of wharf before breakfast, after which I went and took some apartments at the top of Hunter Street, close by Domains. Sydney to me is just like a small London, slums and poor just the same, which you do not see in Adelaide, and the air is very moist and relaxing. Went to James Frazer & Co. and saw Mr. Butchart from whom from whom I obtained my letter, he is a very jolly man.

Tuesday November 22nd.

Went to the Botanical Gardens which are very beautiful, especially the Magnolia, Hibiscus Camdenii and etc. and I enjoyed it much.

Wednesday November 23rd.

Still find the atmosphere too depressing for me, afraid shall have to move. Mallam and self left the wharf at bottom of King Street by steamer at 11.am for Paramatta, we jogged along passing Balmain on our left and St. Leonards on our right then Birchgrove terminating at a point called Longnose, then Greenwich, next to which is the entrance to Lane Cove, where the Paramatta River begins. The steamer then stopped at Bilvela or Cockatoo Island on which is a reformatory school for girls. We next stopped at Hunters Hill passing Drummeroyne and Fire Dock Bay on our left, we next halted at Gladesville with its lunatic asylum on the hill. The village of Ryde was next seen where another halt was made and on the opposite side Homebush with its race course was visible. One more stoppage at Ermington and then at the wharf where we got out for Paramatta. The scenery all the way up the river was very fine and the henbane looked very green after the late rains. The noise the locusts made on the trees was deafening like a lot of sparrows when going to roost. From the wharf a coach took us to Paramatta where we had dinner at the hotel called the 'Woodpecker', then hired a conveyance which took us through the park and very jolly scenery to an orange orchard of 10 acres extent, the oranges and lemons were hanging by hundreds, they were very sweet and nice, we had some given us and also some wine they made called red wine, it is sparkling and like gooseberry wine. The caterpillar is playing great havoc with the vines so that all the vines have to be gone over and the insects picked off. After leaving here, we were taken to the station where we took a train to Sydney being about 16 miles from town.

Thursday November 24th.

Mallam and I took a steam tram from Elizabeth Street and went to Cooger Bay passing through Randwick, with its racecourse which is supposed to be very good. From the end of the tramway we walked about a mile to the beach, all round there are but few houses. The bay is a most delightful spot and the sea was rushing against the rock, made it very pretty. We left in time to get home for dinner.

Friday November 25th.

Went to the museum which is in college street overlooking Hyde Park, the collection of Australian Birds comprises of every known species. There is also a very good collection of fishes, minerals etc.

Sunday November 26th.

Went to the Botanical Gardens this morning and had time to go over them.

Sunday November 27th.

Went to St. Andrews Cathedral to service, the singing was simply awful, not any better than a village choir and not so good as many. Dr. Ellis preached a very good sermon. Captain Ridler from the 'Cuzco' was there. I also spoke to the Purser Mr. Heathcote and one of the mates Mr. Bailey and walked home with them. In the afternoon I called on Mr. and Mrs. Lerick at 'Tarman House', Governor Terrace, Church Hill, then we went for a walk in Hyde Park. They wanted me to tea with them but I felt too seedy.

Monday November 28th.

In the afternoon I called on Mr. and Mrs. Lerick, we went for a walk from the circular quay into the Botanical Gardens, I went back with them and dined there.

Tuesday November 29th.

In the morning I took a steamer from the circular quay to Watson's Bay, the scenery was most captivating and enjoyed the trip especially as it is very close to Sydney, a dull depressing day, but there was a jolly breeze on the water. In the afternoon I called on Mr. Butchard, who invited me to his house next Thursday. I received a letter from home this morning. Lightening very vivid and very beautiful, it lightens up the whole place and is incessant. About 9 pm the thunder was very loud, the lightening became more vivid and we had a terrific storm for about half an hour.

Wednesday November 30th.

In the afternoon I went to the Botanical Gardens to hear the band which plays from 4 pm. to 5 pm. I met Mr. and Mrs. Lerick there and went home with them. Floyer came to wish me goodbye as he has a place at Hadew.

Thursday December 1st.

Called at Frazer & Co for Mr. Butchard and went home with him to his house, had plenty of music and I spent a very pleasant evening, got home about 10.30 pm by bus. Very close and oppressive during the day.

Friday December 2nd.

Mallam still away, does not return until Monday. I took a steamer from Circular Quay to Manley Beach which is a fashionable watering place at the head of Harbour on the left. The township lies between Manley Beach on the Harbour side and Cabbage-Tree Beach on the sea side. The distance between the two is about 2 miles. Passing along the 'Corso' the principal Street you came to Cabbage-Tree beach which is about I mile in length. On one side is 'Curl Curl' Head and on the other is Cabbage-Tree Bay.

Saturday December 3rd.

I took a steamer from Circular Quay and went to Mossmans Bay nearly opposite to Wooloomooloo Bay which is a very pretty place, coming back, a ferry steamer ran down a gentlemen's yacht, the people were taken on board the steamer and then the whole lot transferred to our steamer and taken to Mossmans Bay, so that I had to go back again making a double journey.

Sunday December 4th.

In the morning I went with a young German lady to the Roman Catholic Church, St. Patrics to Mass. The crossing, bowing and antics the Priests coined on were abominable to me, and what with the incense burning, I soon had enough, the singing was however very beautiful and that was what I went there for. In the afternoon we went over the P & O steamer 'Rome', and, what the papers say about her is not an exaggeration, she is a most magnificent vessel, the saloon and wood part is of carved oak or teak, the cabins are as large as those on a sailing vessel, there is everything for comfort and she is in fact a floating palace, she has two funnels and four masts. The crew are all Laskans, and when we went there they were all dressed in white loose trousers with red sash round waist and red turbans and selling mats, coconuts and sticks and they looked jolly sitting down tailor fashion. In the evening I went to St. Andrews Cathedral and the Rev. Vaughan preached a beautiful extemporary sermon, the singing was again beautiful.

Monday December 5th.
Called on Mr. Butchard. Very hot and depressing on account of the moisture.

Tuesday December 6th.
I went with Mallam and Lacey to Sandringham for a drive, we went to Mr. Marks, a friend of Lacey's, who has a jolly place in a park there with beautiful ferns growing by the side of a little stream and it is very pretty. There is also a capital Billiard Room. Very dull depressing day. Mallam returned yesterday. Mallam drove and Lacey used the whip with both hands until they got the animals into a canter which pace he maintained 'till we got home, the only damage was to one of the gateposts at the park entrance which had a piece taken out of it by the wheel. The roads are abominable.

Wednesday December 7th.
I went to Lerick to Cooks River passing through Newtown, the University on the right hand and the Deaf and Dumb Asylum on the left, there is nothing to see at Cooks River. The small farmers out here are called 'Cockatoos' because they never till the ground but scratch and harrow the surfaces.

Thursday December 8th.
A party of six of us went to the North Shore and drove as far as the Half Way House, but did not get any further as it was too foggy to see the beautiful view, we came for and got money from the Bank today.

Friday December 9th.
Lerick and I went to the Mint, first we saw the gold melted, some of the Ingots being worth [POUND]1,500, then it was poured into moulds, the bars being worth on average [POUND]600, next the bars were put between several sets of rollers until they were the proper thickness, then the sovereigns were punched out and are of course quite plain, then they are rounded off, next they are weighed, the light ones going down one tube, and the good ones going down another, the ones that are too heavy down another, the ones that are too heavy and the light ones are melted down again after being weighed, they are

put into a very hot oven and then put into cold water and lastly they are put into a machine where they are stamped and the edges finished off, while they are still soft, it is all done by machinery. They can strike between 15,000 and 20,000 a day. In the afternoon I went and wished the Lericks goodbye. Mrs. Lerick being ill in bed. Wrote to Alfie.

Saturday December 10th.

Went on board the 'Wentworth' Australian Steam Navigation Company and left Circular Quay at 5 pm. Called on Mr. Butchard before I left.

Sunday December 11th.

Head sea and wind, the boat can just make headway, she is a regular old tub, she is as slow as it is possible to get one, this is my first experience of a coasting vessel and hope it will be the last. She shook and tossed about and no mistake and there were only three or four of us on board not queer, there was retching and groaning all round.

Monday December 12th.

Still head sea and wind and still just crawling along.

Tuesday December 13th.

Expected to have been in last night and we ought to have been. Passed Wilsons Promontory about 10.15 am this morning. Passengers still very queer and do not come to meals.

Wednesday December 14th.

Arrived this morning at Sandridge Pier 1 am. Ought to have been in Sunday night. Woke up at 2 am as the Doctor was expected to see that the passengers were all right, false alarm, turned in and roused again at 5 am. Went by the 7 am train to Melbourne and took some rooms by the exhibition. In the afternoon I went to the University Museum, they have a very good collection of Birds, Beasts, Fishes, Reptiles and Insects and have some capital models of Ballarat and other gold mines. They are adding a large piece to the University, the grounds are 40 acres and are laid out well with good walks.

Thursday December 15th.

Went to the Public Library this morning and read, it is a grand place and you can get almost any book you like, there are 97,000 volumes. In afternoon went to the Fitzroy Gardens which extend over 70 acres of land and are laid out beautifully, the fernery is very jolly and contains hundreds of fine fern trees, those from New Zealand being especially good. Fountains, Ponds and Statues are dispensed through the grounds, from these I went to the Treasury Gardens which are also very fine and attractive. The Treasury Buildings and Government Offices are very fine and are far before the buildings of Sydney. The Houses of Parliament are now being completed and bid fair to be a very handsome structure. The General Post Office in Elizabeth Street is one of the finest buildings in the city. There are four Arcades in Bourke Street, Coles Book Arcade being very attractive contains an immense variety of new and second hand books on almost every subject, which was arranged and classified on the shelves. A piano is played from 7pm to 10pm and the arcade is a meeting place for friends.

Friday December 16th.

Had telegram from Sydney from Mallam saying he will be here Thursday. I took a bus to St. Hilda and walked down to the beach, it is a very interesting place. After luncheon went and saw the Cricket Match between "All England Eleven" and Victoria. Bonnor the Australian giant 6 feet 6 inches is one of the Melbourne team.

Saturday December 17th.

Had telegram from Stilling & Co. about 'Hesperus'. Went to the library and read for 2 hours. In the afternoon went to the Cricket Match. Mosquitoes very troublesome and very large.

Sunday December 18th.

Wet. Very seedy, caught cold at match.

Monday December 19th.

Went to the National Gallery, there are some very good pictures, viz. The Brigands, an immense picture in which a gentleman and his wife have been captured by Brigands and there is the old chief with pistol in one hand and paper in the other to be signed so as to get a ransom, the expressions on the faces are very good. Another is 'The Poultry Vendor', a young girl selling Poultry at a stall and a candle burning on the table and the reflections of the light on the girls face are capital. There is also one called a 'Mill Race' by C. J. Lewis representing the mill and mill dam and a person fishing from a point. I do not know whether it is Mr. Lewis of Chelsea. The Statue Gallery is also very good especially the one of The Prince of Wales and there is a splendid collection of models of all the fruits known in Victoria.

Tuesday December 20th.

Sent a letter by the 'Rome'. Had a present of 2 Emu Eggs.

Wednesday December 21st.

Very seedy, obliged to have fire, so cold.

Thursday December 22nd.

Dull day, had a fire again today. Expect Mallam.

Friday December 23rd.

Mallam called today, staying at Scotts. I am still a prisoner, though better.

Saturday December 24th.

Went as far as South Collins Street to see Mallam.

Sunday December 25th.

Of all the miserable things it is to spend a Christmas in Australia, where the sun is blazing hot and you eat your Christmas Dinner at some hotel. The houses are not decorated and they do not keep up Christmas at all excepting in drinking more and they take enough at all times.

Monday December 26th.

Afraid I shall not be able to go to Ballarat with Mallam as arranged. Being a general holiday every possible conveyance is being used from the buggy to a brewers dray.

Tuesday December 27th.

Mallam called, he is going to Geelong. I leave for Adelaide tomorrow by the, 'Catopaxi'.

Wednesday December 28th.

Mallam called this morning, he went with me to the 'Catopaxi', embarked at 1 pm. Dull morning, no sun, warm wind with dust storm, a regular "Brickfielder". Sea very rough, were to have left at 4 pm. but weather prevented. Have cabin to myself and there is hardly room to turn round in it.

Thursday December 29th.

Uneventful day today

Friday 30th December.

Passed Cape Jarvis and Cape Willoughby about 6 pm., anchored at Semaphore about 10.30 pm. Beautiful evening.

Saturday December 31st.

Little Orient boat came about 7 pm and took us off, took train to port and put my heavy luggage on board 'Hesperus' and then took a train to Adelaide and put up again at Murray's. Went to Botanical Gardens where I met Mr. Serle, passenger by 'Catopaxi' and gave me an introductory letter to his uncle at Cape. The atmosphere is beautifully dry, it is delightful. Paid Stilling & Co passage money by 'Hesperus'.

1882

Sunday January 1st.
Went for a walk towards Mitcham, beautifully warm and dry. In afternoon took train to the port and went to see the old vessel.

Monday January 2nd.
Went to the Botanical Gardens, the yellow Acacia in full bloom was very pretty as were also the Magnolia, Bignomia and the Oleandeis of different colours, red, white, yellow, pink, single and double and one mass of blooms.

Tuesday January 3rd.
Met Roland in King William Street. Had a letter from Captain Harry.

Wednesday January 4th.
Met Waring. Sent letter by Orient.

Thursday January 5th.
Took train to Kensington and then went out in the Country, took tram back.

Friday January 6th.
Met Brett. Went to the Institute to see the English Papers.

Saturday January 7th.

Mallam called and dined with me. It is a scorcher today with hot north wind, thermometer in shade 105 degrees fahrenheit, in the sun 166 degrees fahrenheit.

Sunday January 8th.

Hot today but a good deal cooler today. Mr. Murray took me for a long drive round Mitcham, Goodwood and Hyde Park which was very enjoyable, had a capital view of the sea and Adelaide from Mitcham, quite cold this evening.

Monday January 9th.

Temperature in sun 153.5 degrees fahrenheit in shade 95.5 degrees fahrenheit. Mrs. Roland and her son called on me. Had luncheon at the York with Mallam and then went for a drive to Rock Tavern passing between the hills, the scenery was very pretty, there are any number of fruit gardens there, we went on over Mount Lofty, home through Kensington a distance of 15 or 16 miles which was very enjoyable, the old horse went down a cropper, nearly flung us out, fortunately however he only cut one knee a little and grazed his fetlock. Saw Captain Harry at Stillings.

Tuesday January 10th.

Had a tremendous dust storm early this morning, had to get up and shut my window. Met Beywell at Post Office. I embark tomorrow.

VOYAGE HOME
1882

Ship 'Hesperus'.
Skipper:- Captain Harry.
Surgeon:- Mr. Mallam.
Crew:- About 20.

Passengers
Saloon:- 17
2nd. Class:- 24 or 25.

Wednesday January 11th.

Left Adelaide by 1 pm train for Port where tender took us to 'Hesperus' lying off Semaphore, a lot of the old passengers came to see us off. Have a cabin to myself, everything looks just the same and I feel at home.

Thursday January 12th.

Beautifully warm. Skipper came aboard about 1 am (Friday) and then the anchor was weighed and we set sale for England.

Friday January 12th.

Calm. Fine. Saw two sharks close in under the counter in the evening, slight breeze.

Saturday January 14th.
Calm again 'till evening. Passed Cape Borda Lighthouse this evening

Sunday January 15th.
Going at three or four knots, passengers already are ill. A miserable wretch with DTs has been kicking up a dreadful row.

Monday January 16th.
Not much breeze 'till evening. Eight albatrosses flying around, could not catch one. Cold rather in evening.

Tuesday January 17th.
Passengers getting better. Going along well. Very warm and Jolly. Signalled a barque yesterday bound for King Georges Sound, she kept us company for three days, but today she left us behind. There are a tremendous lot of birds on board. Parrots, Cockatoos, Magpies and Laughing Jackasses. The skipper is taking home 200 pairs of Shell Parrots. We have a cargo of wheat, flour, bark and some wool.

Wednesday January 18th.
A very uneventful day, nothing much happened.

Thursday January 19th.
Good winds last two days, rather chilly. Four hundred miles from Cape Servia. Still few passengers at meals. Head sea.

Friday January 20th.
Going about 7 knots an hour. Sea has calmed down a good deal. Squally in afternoon. Signalled the 'Macedon' coasting steamer from Western Australia.

Saturday January 21st.
Only doing 3 or 4 knots an hour. Tried to catch an Albatross but could not.

Sunday January 22nd.
Very bracing day but air rather damp. No service. On wrong course this morning, tacked in afternoon. We have a better lot of passengers than we had coming out.

Monday January 23rd.
Becalmed this morning. Sighted a barque on the starboard side. Rounded Cape Lervin this afternoon. Heavy swell on.

Tuesday January 24th.
Beautifully warm. Sea sickness alright now. Going along steadily.

Wednesday January 25th.
Uneventful day today nothing much happening.

Thursday January 26th.
Going steadily. Nothing now but blue water. Had singing in the evening.

Friday January 27th.
There is a person saloon passenger who mopes about and does not say hardly a word to anyone, always reading the poets, he is called "Gerry alias Shakespeare alias the Philosopher". I sewed up the sleeves of his night shirt.

Saturday January 28th.
Fine fun about Gerry's adventure ship sighted on the starboard side. Becalmed in the afternoon. Very warm. Two of the Mides came into tea this evening, had some music and singing.

Sunday January 29th.
Had service this morning. Only doing 3 knots an hour. Very close and warm out.

Monday January 30th.
Becalmed, sea smooth as a pond, warm. Sunset good this evening. Vessel sighted on port side. Saw some Nautilus this morning.

Tuesday January 31st.
Going very slowly. Skipper reading about Temperance to the passengers, had corrected Mr. Sayer.

Wednesday February 1st.
Have been on board a fortnight today. Lightening up the rigging.

Thursday February 2nd.
Nothing happened of any significance today.

Friday February 3rd.
Have been going along slowly for the last two or three days. Beautifully warm out.

Saturday February 4th.
Very wet all day, had to stay below The doctor reads every afternoon so that time passes.They are trying to get up some charade and concert for next Thursday.

Sunday February 5th.
Had service this morning. Still fine, going only 2 1/2 knots an hour. Ship seen on starboard bow this evening about 9 pm.

Monday February 6th.
Awake last night with tooth ache. A beautiful sunset last evening. Squally afternoon. Poor Muir is in the last stage. I am afraid he will not last through the night.

Tuesday February 7th.
Poor Muir who was suffering from Consumption was seized with Dippnoea yesterday, about 3 pm and did not rally again, he died quietly about 8.30 pm. He was buried this morning at 7 am, the Captain reading the service, it is almost like losing a brother, as he had been on board for 3 weeks and yesterday morning he was laughing and joking. A funeral at sea is very solemn, the body being sewn up in canvas with shot fixed to it and then carried with the Union Jack, when the Captain read "We commit his body to the sea" the First and Second Mate lifted the flag, tilted the body, there was a splash and all was over.

Wednesday February 8th.
Had a rehearsal for tomorrow.

Thursday February 9th.
Had an entertainment this evening.

Programme

Part 1

Overture		Gase and Sayer
Song	Vicars Song	Radcliffe
Song	The Anchors' Weighed	Davis
Song	The White Rose	Mrs. Bulman
Song	Nancy Lee	Captain Harry
Song	The Unfortunate Man	G
Song	The White Squall	McKindley
Duet	The Darkies	Sherwin and Irving

TABLEAUX

Faith Hope and Charity	Jack Horner
Fortune Telling	Whittington and Cat
The Tais Farewell	Beauty and The Beast
The Tais Return	Little Bo Peep

Bluebeard

Part 2

Overture	H Taratore	Sayer and Reid
Song	Minstrel Boy	Tom Phillips
Duet	Larboard Watch	Davis and Vivian
Recitation	Two Verses	Old
Hornpipe		McKindley
Song	Baby Mine	Green
Song	The Englishmen	Davis
Duet	The Darkies	Sherwin and Irvin

God Save the Queen

The entertainment commenced at 8pm and passed off very well indeed. The Tableaux were satisfactory and everybody appeared to like it.

Friday February 10th.

Going along very well. Very damp in the evening. Rolls about a good deal.

Saturday February 11th.

Doing 9 1/2 knots through the night, this morning 7 knots. Beautifully warm out with jolly breeze.

Sunday February 12th.

Had service this morning. Going 8 knots an hour.

Distance 145 miles.

Latitude 27 degrees 43 south.

Longitude 67 degrees 14 east.

Monday February 13th.

Very warm today. Commenced condensing water this morning. Very damp on deck this evening.

Distance 154 miles.

Latitude 28 degrees 05 south.

Longitude 64 degrees 21 east.

Tuesday February 14th.

Some made up Valentines were sent to the girls. Lots of flying fish about, they are larger than I have seen at all.

Wednesday February 15th.

Becalmed all day, we went out in the life boat this morning, it was jolly, the old ship looked fine with all the sails set. Some porpoises about.

Thursday February 16th.

This evening a good breeze sprung up and we are going 12 1/2 knots an hour, the sea is very beautiful, waves breaking over main deck. Scotch mist this morning. Ship on starboard side this evening, off the Mauritius this afternoon.

Friday February 17th.

Beautiful day, jolly breeze and warm, going about 8 knots an hour. Very damp this evening.

Saturday February 18th.

Warm dull day. Speed 5 or 6 knots an hour. Some of the Midies came in to tea.

Sunday February 19th.

Had service this morning. Going very slowly. Beautiful warm evening.

Monday February 20th.

Several long black fish, a kind of whale close alongside of ship. A good sunset this evening.

Tuesday February 21st.

Going well 8 1/2 knots an hour. Ship on starboard side, going same way as we are, we soon left her behind. Splendid warm balmy evening, sat on deck 'till 10 pm.

Wednesday February 22nd.

Uneventful day today nothing of great interest going on.

Thursday February 23rd.
Four vessels in sight, signalled to one of them, going to Bally Straits, Japan. This evening the sailors got up some Christy Minstrels, which was very good, had it on the main deck outside Saloon, which was covered and decorated with flags.

Friday February 24th.
Going along fairly. The vessels are still in sight this morning. I gave the Doctor Chloroform for neuralgia in his eye, after sleeping he was all right.

Saturday February 25th.
Speed 7 knots an hour. Very close and moist. Three sheep have died on the voyage from pneumonia.

Sunday February 26th.
Had no church today as the day is very squally. In the afternoon had a good breeze spring up with rain.

Monday February 27th.
Saw a shark. Two ships in sight on starboard side. Had a game of quoits.

Tuesday February 28th.
Land in sight on starboard side, we are now off Algoa Bay. Very squally with thunder and rain in the afternoon, Albatross, Cape Hens and Gannets travelling about. Some snook about, tried to catch some but could not. Beautiful sunset.

Wednesday March 1st.
Strong breeze running under topsails, sea heavy and beautiful to see the big waves. Glass high.

Thursday March 2nd.

Sea high and very pretty, breaking over deck, going 12 knots an hour. About 3.30 pm we signalled a Yankee Barque on way from Calcutta New York, been out 49 days. The fore Royal split in two, glass gone down a little today.

Friday March 3rd.

Off Cape Agulhas this morning. Running under reefed topsails. Head wind very squally, good sea. The fore topsail split across, also mainsail torn. Sounded this morning, 60 fathoms. The barque 'Oasis' that we signalled to yesterday, is just visible on the port side.

Saturday March 4th.

Signalled to the lighthouse people at Cape Agulhas (12 am.) our name, where from and where to, then all hands were called on deck and the ship was turned about and we went back again. About 5.30 pm. we tacked and had fair wind, in the evening we were becalmed and fished for cod but could not catch any, water too deep, 80 fathoms. Two barques in sight.

Sunday March 5th.

No service this morning. Passed Point Inoin last night and Danger Point this morning at 5 am. Sighted one of Donald Currie's small steam boats. We are close alongside of land, mountains look bare. Any amount of jelly fish of all shapes and colour floating by, they look very pretty. Going at about 1 1/2 knots an hour after being becalmed, (not moving) an inch all morning. There are a lot of gannets or salam geese flying about. Barometer very high, beautiful warm day. One of the barques we sighted yesterday is in sight today. We hope to get in tomorrow about noon.

Monday March 6th.

This morning hardly moving, creeping in slowly. Table Mountain and snow with white clouds hanging over the top of Cape Town at the bottom was grand, as we were entering Table Bay, the 'Sorata' Orient steamer from London passed us. The Ensign was dipped and three cheers given. The anchor was dropped at a quarter to 11 this morning and about 12.30 pm we all went on shore in one of the flat bottomed boats which came off from the shore. On landing we took tram to George's Hotel where we separated, the girls going shopping and the Doctor and I went to Post Office. The Captain arranged to take the girls to Constantia, so Doctor and I said we would go somewhere or other, so we finished our shopping and agreed to meet two of the Midi's at Georges Hotel at 3.30.pm, when we got there, however and we were just going off we met one of the girls who said that the skipper had left them and consequently they could not go to Constantia, so we got another wagonette and a pair to take us, but when the carriages came we found out that nobody had had anything to eat, so that we had to wait for that the skipper having left them to themselves, so that we did not get off 'till about 4.30 pm, at which time we started 5 in one and 7 in the other carriage. The Drive to Constantia was magnificent, very like English scenery with groves of oaks, when we got there we saw the machinery for wine making and tasted some of their red wine which was very good. After that we packed into the traps and drove home by moonlight. It was delightful and beautifully warm. The distance to Constantia is about 14 or 15 miles from town, so that we had a jolly drive, we then put up at 'The Masonic Hotel' where we had some supper, after that the skipper was found about 9 pm. and we started to the wharf for a boat, Mrs. Thomas and Mrs. Creswell having a cab, when we arrived at the wharf we found Miss Thomas and Miss Creswell with the two boys were missing, searching parties namely the Doctor and skipper went off and after about 1 1/2 hours the lost sheep were found and brought back to the wharf when we started for the ship where we arrived at a quarter to 12 pm. being all very tired. A quantity of crayfish were caught by the sailors. Everyone came back laden with the proceeds of their shopping. Cape Town is a very dirty looking place. The Malays and their costumes are very amusing, the women wearing stiff stand out print dresses of different colours, some red, some yellow, green etc., (they must use a lot of starch), then they have a coloured shawl, crossing in front over chest and a gaudy handkerchief twisted over their head, sandals tied on with a piece of twine with a large held between the two first toes. Their babies they carry behind their back, slung by a shawl with just the head out. The majority of Malays go without shoes, although a few wear sandals. The men wear those high brimmed bee-hive hats. Their houses are very small and not over clean. The saloon passengers went off at the Cape and three came on board. Mosquitoes are terrible.

One of the cats fell overboard and the 3rd Mate Puckett jumped over and rescued it, it was just at the last gasp.

Tuesday March 7th.

Scotch mist this morning. The four girls and the doctor on shore this morning shopping and they returned about 2 o'clock. Our new passengers came on board. Had any amount of grapes, 4d. per pound and very good, they were brought to the ship by Malays. A fresh breeze (fair wind) having sprung up. The anchor was weighed at a quarter to 5 pm. and all sail was set and we were once more on our journey to the old country. Sent letters by the 'Conway Castle' bound for England.

Wednesday March 8th.

Have been sailing well all night and this morning we have a fair wind and are gliding along at 10 or 12 knots an hour, she rolls a good deal, as there is a cross sea running, the waves are very pretty, some of the men got washed out of their bunks in the forecastle. Some of the passengers are sea sick again. Out of sight of land now. Had some fresh fish and fruit for breakfast which was a treat. very chilly.

Thursday March 9th.

Rolled tremendously last night, kept me from sleeping and this morning is nearly as bad, you have to look out for legs of mutton in your lap at dinner. Going at about 12 knots. It is a good deal warmer. Heavy sea still.

Friday March 10th.

Steamer passed on starboard side about 10 O'clock last night. Going along 10 knots an hour. The cat that Puckett saved from drowning on Monday night died from the effects of water in its lungs. The sister cat has a piece of black crepe round neck in memorandum. Ship jolly and steady. This morning sea gone down a good deal since yesterday.

Saturday March 11th.

I took to smoking again after having left it off for eighteen days, I was not any better without it and the Doctor told me to take to it again and I was very glad of it. Two of the Midi's came into tea this evening. Going along at 10 knots an hour.

Sunday March 12th.

Had service this morning, very small congregation. Dull, close day without sun. We are now in the tropics. Doing about 7 knots an hour and we hope to get to St. Helena Thursday morning. Jolly dry evening.

Monday March 13th.

Close and moist this morning with but little sun. The doctor vaccinated the baby and himself and then did me. Going along about the same as yesterday.

Tuesday March 14th.

Barque on the port side, speed about 5 knots. Rather close in day time, but a beautiful evening. Had a game of whist.

Wednesday March 15th.

They are scraping the old paint off ship already for painting her again, have tarred the rigging. Ship very steady, going at 5 knots. Nothing fresh going on.

Thursday March 16th.

Land sighted this evening about 6.30 pm. Not going very fast.

Friday March 17th.

Sails taken in and anchor was dropped at quarter to 9 am. There is nothing but bare rocks to be seen with the town between the hills. The girls and the Captain went on shore about 9 am. and I went about half an hour later and met them in town. It is the most horrible place I have ever seen, the houses are small and dirty, there are no shops to get anything and nothing but black beggars everywhere. There was a jolly little child about 4 years old which I tried to buy to bring back to the old country, but the mother would not part with him, the ladies said the child was like me, so I had to go and see it, they kissed him and fondled him and I said that I did not see why I should not be served the same, but they have not done it yet. There were any amount of black men and women came on board with junk and curios. The skipper took the girls to Longmore to see Napolians grave, they got on board about 7 pm. when we had dinner. There are about a dozen Yankies Whalers at anchor now. The 93rd Regiment is stationed here now.

Saturday March 18th.

The Captains' gone ashore. The Doctor took the Girls and Mr.and Mrs. Grainger on shore and then went for a drive, I did not go. They returned about 6 pm. We had eight young ladies and one gentleman to dinner and they had a dance on the Poop and went away about 10. pm, they had not much beauty. I was standing on the gangway talking to young Peterson, 18 years of age and to Will. Eccremont 14 years old when some of the people took me to be the father of these two boys (a widower). I must look ancient. It is a wretched close moist day, anything but pleasant. Discharging cargo all day. any amount of blacks on board with fruits etc.

Sunday March 19th.

The Captain has taken Miss Annie Thomas and Miss Emma Cresswell to dine with the Bishop and the Doctor has gone to church with Maggie Thomas and Lillie Cresswell. We had the American Consul to luncheon, he is a fat merry old chap. Very close and dull. The 'Durban' came in about 9 pm. and anchored close alongside of us and left about 12 pm. The skipper went on board to take letters. Had the face ache that I was obliged to have two Hypodermic Injections of Morphia.

Monday March 20th.

The skipper, The Doctor and all the girls went on board a whaler in the afternoon, and after they had gone I took Annie Thomas on board the 'Milton', another whaler and when we got there we found there was only ropes to get on deck, so I spoke to the mate and he sent a man up to the main yard to fix a pulley to it and then let down a chair with a new flag spread over it and we went up, it was fine. We went down in the Captain's Cabin which was very small, but comfortable. We then saw the harpoons, lances and guns for firing the lances and also for explosive bullets. After we had seen everything we were let down in our chair and went to our old ship. There were a lot of ladies and gentlemen came to luncheon and they were not up to much. Had another injection of Morphia last night which made me happy. In the evening went on shore and came back at 10.30 pm.

Tuesday March 21st.

Two whalers, one was at anchor and the other going out and ran into the one at anchor, but not much damage was done. Puckett, third mate had an ugly squeeze at his knee between a cask full of molasses and the iron rail, his knee is bruised a good deal but no bones are broken. The Doctor took Mrs.Thomas and daughter and Miss Cresswell on shore and came back to luncheon. A lot more black people came on board to sell things. The 'Barbarossa' and 'South Australian', ships anchored about mid-day, the latter one from Adelaide leaves this evening so that it will be a race. About 5 pm. we weighed anchor and then set sail, the Ensign being hoisted at stern and away we went after three cheers had been given to the people on the 'South Australian' which was answered. We had a good breeze to carry us out and I am jolly glad to see the last of that horrible island. Had an injection of Morphia last night. Was on deck late last night as it was so hot on board. We took in a few tons of cargo and discharged about 200 or 300 tons. We also took in some fowls and fruit.

Wednesday March 22nd.

Going at about 8 knots an hour. Cleaning and painting ship. A cask of molasses broke and went all over the place. We are now a foot more out of the water, now we have got rid of our St. Helena cargo. Had a squally evening.

Thursday March 23rd.

Going about 8 knots. Had a morphia hypodermic injection last night, but did not sleep a wink. Tuesday there was a jolly row because Annie Thomas did not go with the rest to the whaler, but afterwards went with me to one. The Doctor went on shore and said he was going to sleep there, but he came back at 10 pm. Old Mrs.Thomas and her other daughter were crying and there was a rumpus yesterday, Annie Thomas went and said she was sorry and kissed and so satisfied the doctor and the old girl. Splendid evening, not damp in the least.

Friday March 24th.

Going at about 6 knots an hour. There is a rumpus now because the girls were on deck with us and the old skipper was jealous. Had injection of morphia.

Saturday March 25th.

Close and dull weather. On deck up to 10.30 pm. Some of the Midi's asked in to tea.

Sunday March 26th.

The Island of Ascension sighted early this morning and we passed it about 6. pm. in the evening, it is a government station and very barren, we saw a ship going there. Any amount of Topsey Turvey Birds or sea swallows came from the island. Saw some black fish this morning. Had service this morning. Very hot, close and moist.

Monday March 27th.

Very hot and close. Had morphia injection last two nights. Flying fish and black fish knocking about.

Tuesday March 28th.

Dreadfully close and moist. Going along very slowly. Sailors getting on with the painting etc. Had three quarters of a grain of morphia injected last night, but did not sleep. Some porpoises came alongside of ship.

Wednesday March 29th.

Last night went to bed about 10 pm. Got up and went on deck about 11 pm, it being so hot in cabin, could not sleep, so I had a cigar about 1 am. and then went to sleep for an hour, then came down into my bunk again, but slept very little, it being so dreadfully hot. Thermometer on deck up to 80 degrees fahrenheit.

Thursday March 30th.

Going along very slowly. A ship astern of us. There was a proper row today between Mrs.Thomas and the Doctor, just because Maggie Thomas had hysteria and the Doctor talked to her and brought her alright again and the fat old dame being jealous insulted the Doctor, before all the passengers on the poop and the consequences are that Maggie and Annie Thomas are not to speak to him, nor will the old dame, she is entirely wrong and ought to have apologised to the Doctor. Had injection of morphia last night.

Friday March 31st.

A vessel on the port side today. The fat old virago of Mrs.Thomas was bullying Maggie all day and in the evening because someone spoke to Maggie when she was crying the old lioness flew into an awful rage and dragged Maggie to the other side of deck and behaved in a disgraceful manner. I shall not speak to the virago anymore. The Captain gave her a good talking to, so that now she allows her daughters to speak to the Doctor. Had an injection of morphia and an opium pill. No name is bad enough for a woman like that and it was simply because she was jealous of the Doctor talking to her daughters and thought that he ought to spoon with her. Had morphia.

Saturday April 1st.

Very close and sultry, squally in afternoon. Going along very slowly.

Sunday April 2nd.

Did not have any service, on account of it being so squally, in the morning going at 12 1/2 knots an hour and in the evening going at 3 1/2 knots. Dreadfully close, no cool place to get to. Nearly all the passengers are sea sick again. We crossed the like this morning.

Monday April 3rd.

Becalmed this morning. Very moist and dreadfully close, Can hardly breathe, shall be very glad to get out of the duldrums. Two outward bound vessels on port side. In the evening going from 2 to 3 knots.

Tuesday April 4th.

Rained heavily last night. Had some morphia injected. Becalmed again all day. Very close and moist. Sea smooth as a mill pond. A lot of the birds die this hot weather, about 200 have died since leaving Adelaide. Had morphia injection.

Wednesday April 5th.

This morning about 3 am. it rained proper tropical rain, it did not come down in drops but like pouring it out of buckets to about mid-day, it cleared up. Going along 3 knots an hour. It is a good deal cooler today, hope it will keep so. The Doctor speaks to the virago Mrs.Thomas, I don't. Have been on board 12 weeks today. Had injection of morphia.

Thursday April 6th.

Becalmed all the morning until about 2 pm, a breeze sprung up and we were going 4 knots an hour. A lot of albacores about. Had a Tam-O-Shanter made me, also a woolen skull cap. Very close. Had morphia. We blew bubbles in the evening.

Friday April 7th.

Good Friday today. Young Peterson a precocious youth from the cape kissed Emma Creswell last evening and this morning she is cut up about it, so there is a jolly row. There is any amount of jealousy among the girls and old Mother Thomas over the Doctor and he enjoys the lark, it is great fun. The virago being able to squeeze out a few crocodile tears whenever she likes. Going along 5 knots an hour, rather close. A black fish came in pretty close to the ship. An outward bound vessel on the port side some distance away.

Saturday April 8th.

Going along 6 or 7 knots an hour. Men getting on with the painting. The sea was pretty this evening, being one mass of phosphorous astern.

Sunday April 9th.

Lot of passengers are sea sick again. Going along 10 1/2 knots last night and this morning about 8 knots. Did not have service today. A flying fish flew on board. It is much cooler today.

Monday April 10th.

Still going along well. An outward bound barque passed us on the starboard side. Had a game of whist this evening.

Tuesday April 11th.

Doing 11 knots an hour during the night and this morning we are going 10 knots. Saw some porpoises close by side of the ship. Cooler today but the air is moist and damp.

Wednesday April 12th.

Breeze still keeps up. Going at 8 1/2 knots this morning. Still close and moist.

Thursday April 13th.

Good breeze. Very seedy today, had a wretched nigh, no sleep at all. The girls read to me. Captain had a tea party in his cabin, I did not go as I was so queer, had tea by myself. The Doctor and I had a game of cribbage. I did not have an injection of morphia last night, after having it every night since March 20th.

Friday April 14th.

Had an injection of morphia last night and so had a quiet night and am better today. Going along well. A barque passed us on the starboard side bound for West Indies. Annie Thomas read to me 'The Jumping Frog' this morning. Jolly cool with sun.

Saturday April 15th.
Going along about 6 knots an hour. The sails were singing all evening.

Sunday April 16th.
Had service this morning and there were very few there. Going only about 1 knot. We are now out of the tropics. It is a very pleasant day. I was lying in the Doctors hammock all afternoon and he read to me one of Longfellow's poems.

Monday April 17th.
Going along very slowly. The girls read to me. Sun warm. It was a splendid sunset this evening. A barque on the port side.

Tuesday April 18th.
Hardly moving today. A vessel bound for America on starboard side. Some of the sailors caught a dolphin. The sailors were singing all the evening. They are now painting on the poop.

Wednesday April 19th.
Going along about 4 1/2 knots an hour. Sun very hot. Southern Cross is no hardly visible. The Doctor read to me last night from 10.30 pm. 'till 12.pm. I did not get any sleep. Poor Granger is very queer with asthma, he has been in his cabin for the last three days. We hope to get home the first week in May. Had an injection of morphia each day since last Friday.

Thursday April 20th.
Beautiful sunrise this morning. Going about 1 knot an hour this morning, but after 12 O'clock there was a squall and we had more wind, but off our course, went about ship and turned around at 6 pm. and then had fair wind. Going 6 or 7 knots an hour. In the evening it rained tremendously. Had morphia injection. Two ships sighted on port side.

Friday April 21st.

Fair wind but head sea, going along 8 1/2 knots an hour. Rolling a good deal. A steamer outward bound passed us. This morning our starboard side passengers are sea sick again. Had morphia injection 1/2 grain.

Saturday April 22nd.

Speed 8 knots an hour. A vessel on the port quarter. Quite chilly now. Had morphia injection 1/4 grain.

Sunday April 23rd.

Had service this morning. Going about 10 knots all day. A homeward bound brig on starboard side. Warm with a jolly breeze. Morphia injection 1/6 grain.

Monday April 24th.

Rolled about tremendously during night, wind being aft and has dropped a good deal so we are only going 3 knots an hour. Beautiful sunny day. Homeward bound brigantine on port side. The sea looks a darker colour now. We are nearing the Western Islands. Have been 101 days today. The retriever dog belonging to one of the quartermasters died this morning.

Tuesday April 25th.

Splendid day going along 4 knots an hour. Sailors are varnishing the poop. Vessel on starboard side. Expect to get home about the 6th or 7th of next month. Hypodermic injection of morphia 1/3 grain.

Wednesday April 26th.

Going about same as yesterday. Beautiful warm day with clear blue sky. The old virago has been at it again, she has been bullying Emma Cresswell, because she went for a walk with the Doctor and the old cat was jealous. Three of the boys came into tea this evening. Had morphia 1/3 grain.

Thursday April 27th.

Going about 5 knots an hour. Vessels on port side. We have now passed the last of the Western Islands viz. Flores and Coiro, they were sighted early this morning and about 4 pm. we had passed Flores and at 6.30 pm Coiro was passed, they are both inhabited. A lot of gulls followed us from the islands. Had morphia 1/3 grain. Some of the boys came into tea. Had a rubber of whist.

Friday April 28th.

Going well during the night and this morning there is a good south westerly breeze and we are going along 8 knots an hour. Dull, cloudy, cold and bracing day, regular English weather,. Several vessels in sight. In the afternoon had rain. Morphia injection 1/3 grain.

Saturday April 29th.

Going about the same pace as yesterday. A brigantine in sight on starboard bow. Some porpoises close alongside of vessel. Too cold to sit about on deck now, have to keep moving. We have every sail set this morning. The wind has shifted more to the west and our course is east by north ears.

Sunday April 30th.

At 10 pm. last night we were going at 12 knots an hour. During the middle watch it was very squally, had to shorten sail, the crotchet split in two, she was healing over on her side. This morning going between 8 and 9 knots an hour, very squally. Very cold especially before a squall. A whaler in sight this morning on starboard side which passed very soon. Glass going down a little so there is a chance of this wind carrying us into the channel. Last night Mrs.Granger dressed up as a man. I had a nasty fall on my face the deck being so slippery. Had morphia 1/3 grain.

Monday May 1st.

Very squally night. Going 11 or 12 knots the whole time, she heels over a good deal and this morning she rolls tremendously. Going about 8 knots an hour, wind gone back, is nearly dead aft now. We have to go without a crotchet now, have not another. Some porpoises alongside of vessel. Glass going down steadily. You have to look out at meal times or else you get a leg of mutton or cup of tea in your lap now the vessel rolls so. Some of the passengers are ill again. In the evening very squally and went to north east, worst luck. Had morphia 1/3 grain.

Tuesday May 2nd.

This morning at 6 am. shortened sail and reefed topsail as there was a gale of wind from north east blowing, a little later the wind freshened, we stood to the east only under the top sail (lower) on each mast and the vessel rolling a good deal, the sea however is not heavy. As the sailors were furling the upper topsail on foremast, one of the apprentices poor little Myers was helping, he let go a minute to warm his hands, when the ship gave a lurch and he fell backwards from the topsail yard onto the forecastle rail and then onto the main deck, injuring his spine and skull, I am afraid there is not much chance for him, he is now unconscious and his legs are paralysed. The top sail was split this morning. Have had to stay below all day, as there has been a squall about every 1/2 hour and the wind is piercing coming from the north east. Smoking and reading in the Doctors cabin. About 8 of us for dinner today and you have to hold on to things or they will come onto your lap. A lot of little grey gulls, channel pilots as the sailors call them are following the ship. The glass is rising, so hope the wind will die out and that we shall get a fair wind soon. The skipper says that they are having rough weather in the channel.

Wednesday May 3rd.

Myers is still alive in an unconscious state. Very wet and cold. I stopped in the Doctors Cabin all day with him smoking and reading. Morphia 1/3 grain.

Thursday May 4th.

Going on slowly. Still cold, have to keep walking about in the evening. Small rain. Morphia 1/4 grain. In soundings.

Friday May 5th.

Going slowly this morning, 150 miles from Lands End. Five barques a brig and a homeward bound steamer in sight. Wind very cold. Myers is just about the same. The Doctor wrote a poem on the passengers on board. The vessel is now very steady all canvas set. Morphia 1/2 grain.

Saturday May 6th.

Becalmed all day, sea like a mill pond. A lot of steamers and vessels all round us. We are now off the Scilly Islands. A pilot came off in a boat from a cutter, quite a treat to see a boat on the sea again, looks as if we are near land. Signalled the 'Cypuan' steamer came close.. Miss Thomas read to me. Morphia 1/3 grain.

Sunday May 7th.

Myers is conscious this morning. We are now standing in for the Lizard, hope soon to get good wind. Steamers and vessels any amount. Had tooth ache very badly last night. No service today. The pilot who came on board yesterday said that last Sunday and Monday they had the strongest gale from south west, that has been known for years (confirming what the Captain said last Tuesday). A man of war training ship passed us this morning about 11 am. We had a fair wind and this afternoon we are going 5 1/2 knots an hour. Was in the Doctors cabin smoking and taking it easy all the afternoon. Sighted the Lizard 8.40 pm. and the Start Point Light at 10 pm.

Monday May 8th.

Passed Portland and St. Albans Head this morning before luncheon and can see The Needles and St. Katherine Point. Have a nice little breeze. Any amount of steamers and sailing vessels. Two barques viz. the 'Planter' and 'Forfairshire' signalled to us yesterday to be reported. Beautiful clear day with sunshine. The sea of a beautiful green. Myers is better today and gives hope of recovery now. Off the Needles at 1 pm. and passed Ventnor, Shanklin and before dinner took a tug boat which was homeward bound, was not powerful enough so took us very slowly.

Tuesday May 9th.

Passed Beach Head at 3 am. Hastings and St. Leonards before breakfast and off Dungeness about 11 am. where we took a pilot and also another tug boat and Dover, South Forland, Ramsgate, North Foreland and Margate before tea. Any amount of vessels, steamers and others. Saw French coast opposite Dover very plainly.

Wednesday May 10th.

Arrived at Gravesend a little after 3 am. this morning, got our letters. I went off very soon to part with the old ship, enjoyed my voyage very much and has done me good. Left Waterloo by 2.30 pm. train for home where I arrived about 5 pm. The end of my jolly voyage.

POEM BY DR. MALLAM

"HESPERUS" MAY 7th. 1882.

The clipper ship 'Hesperus' started homeward bound.
From Adelaide in January, all so safe and sound.
And as she spread her canvas and got before the wind.
Gently down the Gulf we sailed with contented mind,
For had we not a Captain on whom we could rely.
For careful navigation with wakeful watchful eye,
The name of "Harry" is enough full confidence to give,
To friends at home as well as those with him about to live.
For stimulants of all kinds he wisely does eschew.
So is always at his post when there is anything to do,
They thought they caught him nipping once when all alone.
But Oh! dear no, t'was not champagne but only zoldone.
Tobacco and snuff are alike unknown.
Will not this account for the length his beard has grown,
Or is it due to stroking a habit he's acquired.
Or due to gentle cultivation because so much admired.
The ladies think it lovely and becoming to the face,
And combined with the moustache gives to the features grace.
And may be 'tis so there the eye with merry twinkle glowing,
Makes me think 'tween me and you he must be very knowing.
I don't think there is much goes on but what he knows about.
Ant the men all fear when he goes near to talk, at least to shout.
One thing more and then with Captain we have done.

His laugh 'tis loud, not musical and not always denotes fun,
It may be heard from morn 'till night, from poop to quarter deck.
And at its loudest starts suspicion someone's peace 'tis bent to wreck.
Kindest of men and thoughtful no wonder he's so popular.
The ladies all both great and small love him, he's so jocular.

Next come the officers chief of which a canny Scott is he.
Tall and erect, broad shouldered and fearless as can be.
He sticks not at trifles, loves his chaff and many a yarn can spin.
And with such a serious face but beware don't take all you hear in.
His hair is short and curley, his complection ruddy and Oh!
I forgot to mention his appellation 'tis George Monro.
The second mate is a curious man, most good natured and kind,
Short and dark, thin and sallow but a man with a very big mind.
His silent perambulations when 'tis his watch on deck.
Help by their uncertain directions to hold many in check.
And his voice is subdued and whispering and he has an air of mystery.
As of some crime guilty, discoverable as likely very.
And as for his amatureness his heart he loses every cruise.
In fact I think his time is drawing near for he can't have much more to lose.
Puckett the 3rd. mate is a very noisy boy with round face and chubby red,
A dark blue eye and hairless face and a fellow who likes to be fed.
Liberal and open handed and glad to do you a turn.
Quick, hasty and round and a fire within that can burn.
But the fire is soon put out and then you should hear him sing.
A happy disposition but he must always be on the wing.

And what of the 4th mate, face the little Prince in disguise.
He certainly has a superior cut at times looks awfully wise.
A very nice fellow, a little proud with a failing most common to man.
Every man for himself he says, and a good turn if you can.

Apprentices 5 who live in our den and pretty well agree,
Their names are Vivian, Walduck, Myers, Swain and little Dothie.

But we must pass on to the passengers who form so large a part.
Their funny ways and manners intrigues of heart.
Young and old, great and small in all 14 in all we mustered.
And I'll attempt to describe them as round our table clustered.

Mrs.Thomas then comes 1st. a widow stout and very comely.
Seventeen stone they say she weighs, and she is extremely homely.
Her son Evan "A mothers boy" aged 15 and rather spoiled.
Would at public school do well, but I fear this plan is foiled.
For mater ne'er could part with him and the drill would be severe.
As in England he must for at least three long year.
Daughters 2 are also with her going home to see the land.
Where their father and their mother first began to run life's old sand.
Maggie aged 20 is quiet, reserved an invalid has been,
Is looked upon as proud by many and as very cold I ween,
But this is not so for you break this crust of ice.
And then you'll find her warm within and also very nice.
Annie is her sister on whom you may rely,
A jolly girl, good looking and one who makes you sigh.
Never out of temper but a smile for all has she.
And every bit of mischief at the bottom of will be.
A little boy is with them Willy Acreman by name,
14 a dear good hearted boy who is always just the same.
A plucky manly little chap who to educate is bound.
I wish him well with all my heart and back both safe and sound.

Mrs.Creswell is a widow whom the world has handled badly.
Very active for her years but looking rather pale and sadly,
Grown wise by tribulation, she has learnt to treat things lightly.

And rheumatism is the only thing that disturbs her nightly.
Emma Creswell is a comical girl, exceedingly fond of the boys,
And I'm sure they're fond of her and "by George" give her many joys.
A fine tall girl attractive too with eyes Oh! such a pair.
No wonder heads are turned by her and then look at her hair,
Of delicate attentions in silver, gold and shell.
I'm sure she has enough of them to prove she is a bell.
Her sister Lilly has been called the fairest flower that blows,
And I quite agree with them and as everybody knows.
A lover she has waiting her so let us all beware.
I trust her future may be bright and free from every care.
Mr.Sayer the man of diamonds, what of him can I say.
He is thin and tall, meish looking and his bill can always pay.
But he has a wicked way not becoming of his years,
Of romance setting people by the ears.
From his own account believe me he has led a funny life,
And now is never happy but in stirring up some strife.
Of his wife I know no more when at the Cape we parted,
Than at starting was she shy? or not at least open hearted.
For mischief were they rife to lies at times resorted,
But the maidens would not quarrel and so the scheme they aborted.
Dr Clay a quiet fellow, well meaning and free from vice.
Good tempered, merry and pleasing in fact most awfully nice.
Eyes most terribly wicked, he's convalescing from lung disease.
With a troublesome cough and weak thus! by no means hard to please.
I think you may roam the world o'er and a difficult matter 'twill be,
To find one more harmless and gentle and from affection free.

Poor Muire a plucky consumptive was fated to leave us soon,
And his relief from suffering must surely be a boon.
But we deeply geared to lose him and trust he's gone above.
To reap the reward of those whose religion is one of love.

Fancy a tall pale man with great big hands and feet.
Large grey eyes and languid who oft abstained from meat.
Pea soup he much enjoyed and vegetable diet.
His own society too and perfect rest and quiet.
For the girls a butt he proved and they never let him rest.
But we're always poking fun or else some merry jest.
So they teased his very life and made him most unhappy.
But he was not so very green or such an awful sappy.
For he rounded on them in earnest with a kiss.
On the poop on Sunday night which for him was not amiss.
And then the man had rest and glad he was Oh! very.
Mr.Radcliffe was his name tho' you know him as "Jerry".
He left us at the Cape very tired of our society.
Going quickly home by steam on account of the variety.

Miss Davis poor woman was for our example was she sent.
By rheumatism crippled and her joint most sorely bent.
Ever patient under suffering unselfish, always bright.
We carry all our griefs to her, she always sets us right.
By some she's called a sunbeam a rare good woman surely.
One who wins your heart by sympathy most purely.
At the Cape we took some passengers, A Mr.and Mrs.Granger.
And also Freddy Peterson tho' of him we made no stranger.
For he soon fell into our ways a lad of tender age.
He was taken by the belle who did engage.
To look after him and care for him from home so far away.
If he would only care for her and proper homage pay.
The other were two invalids, Mr.G. with asthma bad,
And Mrs.G., Oh! those mosquitoes they nearly drove her mad.
But the spots they soon got better and getting accustomed to the sea.
We found her bright and lively and very mischievous was she.
Her husband poor fellow suffered much and needed aid.

And a rare good woman she proved and every attention paid.
Their nights were much disturbed and nitre paper lighted.
And I don't think he'll get better until England we have sighted.
And now the sad end is approaching, we cast an eye o'er the past.
How have we suited each other and are friendships likely to last.
Of one thing I am certain, the Colonials are very kind,
And set us a brilliant example in many things you'll find.
We will receive them with open arms and make their time so jolly.
In innocent amusements omitting all the folly.
That pleasant recollections they may have of England's shore.
We wish them happiness both now and ever more.

By Miss Davis

Your verses are pleasing but with your kind permission,
We would just like to notice a most serious omission.
Where's our dear friend the Doctor and what has he done,
To be left out in the cold while we have the fun.
Of all our ships company he takes the lead.
In all kindest actions and unselfish deeds.
Dr Mallam his name a "Guys Man" so clever.
And we all agree he's a wonderful treasure
With eyes one can trust, suggestive of willingness.
Whilst disclosing a heart brimming over with tenderness.
We think over sensitive but that's only a reminder.
We have grieved him perhaps when we might have been kinder.
But we know he forgives them, how nicely he reads to us.
Serves afternoon tea, strong with cows milk, delicious.
A charming arrangement introduced by the Doctor,
And often accompanied with much fun and laughter.
We value his friendship and shall keep it in store.
Long after our shipmates are settled on shore.
And though at our parting thoughts may be unspoken.
We trust that his friendship will never be broken.

("Hesperus" May 8th 1882)

www.ingramcontent.com/pod-product-compliance
Lightning Source LLC
Chambersburg PA
CBHW070543300426
44113CB00011B/1776